19 32

D0535586

DISCARDED
Richmond Public Library

Notes of a White Black Woman

Notes of a

White Black Woman

Race
Color
Community

Judy Scales-Trent

The Pennsylvania State University Press
University Park, Pennsylvania

31143006112271
305.8009 Sca
Scales-Trent, Judy.
Notes of a white Black
woman : race, color, and
community

Library of Congress Cataloging-in-Publication Data

Scales-Trent, Judy.
    Notes of a white black woman : race, color, community / Judy
Scales-Trent.

        p.   cm.
    Includes bibliographical references.
    ISBN 0-271-01430-X (alk. paper)
    1. Race awareness — United States.   2. Color of man — Social as-
pects — United States.   3. Afro-Americans — Race identity.
4. Racism — United States.   5. United States — Race relations.
6. Scales-Trent, Judy.   7. Afro-Americans — Biography.   8. Afro-
American women — Biography.   I. Title.
E185.625.S26   1995
305.8'00973 — dc20   94-45176
                                                                    CIP

Copyright © 1995 The Pennsylvania State University
All rights reserved
Printed in the United States of America

Published by The Pennsylvania State University Press,
University Park, PA 16802-1003

It is the policy of The Pennsylvania State University Press to use acid-
free paper for the first printing of all clothbound books. Publications
on uncoated stock satisfy the minimum requirements of American National Standard for Information Sciences — Permanence of Paper for
Printed Library Materials, ANSI Z39.48–1984.

for my mother
Viola Scales Trent

and for the memory of my father
William J. Trent Jr.
1910–1993

Contents

Introduction

We Americans have been talking about race for a long time. It is a constant theme in our lives and in our common language. Although the specific topic changes over the years — varying all the way from fugitive slave laws to affirmative action — the theme remains. Ideas about race lie at the core of the American character and the American dream.

In general, discussions about race center on the state of relations between black Americans and white Americans. They focus on who will control the resources: freedom, jobs, schools, housing, medical care. In some of this debate, black people call white people mean and ignorant and hateful, and white people call black people the same. At other times, we wonder whether there will ever be harmony between the races, and whether there is anything we can do to hasten the arrival of that day. Groups that might appear to be outside this debate are nonetheless connected to it. For example, people ask how Jews situate themselves with respect to the black-white drama: Which side are they on? How about Native peoples? And what does it mean that there will be more Mexican Americans than African Americans by the year 2010? How will that affect the great black/white racial divide so familiar to us all? Among the millions of Americans who participate in this discussion, points of view differ drastically. There seems to be profound agreement, however, with the notion that race is a serious matter in America, and always has been.

The most important premise of these discussions is the existence of "race" itself. We all simply know that "race" exists. It is obvious, it is real, it has its own independent presence. You can just look around and see how the world is split up — black people sitting over there at that table, white people walking together down that hall, maybe a table with black people and white people sitting together. Our eyes tell us this truth. Thus, racial identity is simply assumed. It is not questioned. It is not noticed or seen or discussed. It just is.

In these essays, I take my place in the debate on racial matters in America by moving the discussion back a step, to talk about the creation of "race" itself. What do we mean by "race" in this country? How is "race" created? Who creates it? How is racial identity maintained? What is the law of racial purity that America uses to create and maintain racial identity? And how does it work? I address these questions by showing the operation of America's racial purity law on my life — that is, on the life of one American.

Because I am a black American who is often mistaken for white, my very existence demonstrates that there is slippage between the seemingly discrete categories "black" and "white." This slippage is important and can be helpful to us, for it makes the enterprise of categorizing by race a more visible — hence, a more conscious — task. It is at this point, then, that we can pause and look carefully at what we are doing. It is at this point of slippage that we can clearly see that "race" is not a biological fact but a social construct —

and a clumsy one, at that. Stories about my life as a white black American also show that creating and maintaining a racial identity takes a lot of effort on my part, and on the part of other Americans. "Race" is not something that just exists. It is a continuing act of imagination. It is a very demanding verb.

Many are surprised to discover that America has racial purity laws. We know that Nazi Germany and South Africa once did. Some even know that such formal, written laws existed in America from the earliest days of the colonies through at least the 1980s. One example is Virginia's 1924 law, which says:

> The term "white person" shall apply only to the person who has no trace whatsoever of any blood other than Caucasian, but persons who have one-sixteenth or less of the blood of the American Indian, and no other non-Caucasic blood shall be deemed white persons.

But racial purity laws would have to exist in this country, as they do in every culture that uses racial definitions: where race is important, there must be a way to sort by race. Thus, to the extent that we talk about race in America, we are basing our talk on notions of racial purity. The concept of race cannot exist without the concept of racial purity.

The need for racial purity laws arose in America as soon as an African and a European had sexual relations here and produced a child. Was the child African? European? Something else? It is not surprising, then, that the question was raised early. At the beginning of the seventeenth century, when sexual contact between these two groups took place, it was generally between enslaved and free blacks, and white indentured servants, in the colonies of Maryland and Virginia. Initially, the status of these relationships — and of the children born of these relationships — was uncertain. But by 1662 the state of Virginia, troubled by these relationships, passed its first law banning miscegenation.

By the early 1700s, the upper South had begun to formulate the social rule that held that all children with African ancestry would be considered "black." In making this decision, white Southerners rejected several other possibilities. For example, they could have considered these children "white"; they could have created a third racial category; and indeed, they could have eliminated the concept of race altogether. Instead, the upper South decided that the taint of Africa was so strong that one ancestor from Africa ("one drop of black 'blood'") would mark a child "black." (This rule is popularly called "the one black ancestor rule" or "the 'one-drop' rule"; anthropologists call it "hypodescent," which means that racially mixed people are assigned the status of the subordinate group. This rule applies only to African Americans in the United States and apparently also exists only in this country.) Early on, support for this rule spread throughout the South. Eventually this social norm was codified into law.

The laws, however, were not uniform. They varied from state to state; they often varied, as well, within a given state over time. Hence, a person might be white in one state and black in another. Or a person might be black under state law one day, and the next day white — or vice versa. Nonetheless, well before the Civil War the "one-drop rule" was widespread in the North and in most of the South. Today, although as a general rule racial purity laws are no longer codified in formal laws, they have not disappeared. They remain in effect as very strong social norms in the United States. And the "one-drop rule" of racial purity is generally accepted by both black and white communities in America.

That is a brief history of the development and spread of the rule of hypodescent, which controls racial identity in America today. It is important to realize, however, that the creation and enforcement of this rule has had a powerful effect not only *on* the African American community but also *within* the African American community. In order to understand the impact of this rule within the African American community, we must return to the plantations.

As slavery developed in the black-belt plantations, owner-ship of African women soon included owning their sex life also. Thus, it was common for African women who were enslaved to be sexually assaulted, raped, made concubines. It was also common for the master (or other males in the mas-ter's family) to bring a particular slave woman to live and work in his home, in order to facilitate his sexual attacks. One result of this move to the master's house was that these enslaved women — and the children they had with the slave owners — were in close enough contact with European Amer-icans to learn their language, habits, and beliefs. Some of the children were able to gain an education; the boys were often apprenticed to artisans, from whom they learned skilled trades. This did not mean that these women and children were not still slaves and still treated cruelly, but it did mean that members of the slave master's black family were often able to acquire certain skills because they lived in close prox-imity to the slave master's white family. Indeed, some slave owners freed the children they had with slave women.

These skills became an important way for slaves to find extra work, and thus earn enough money to buy their free-dom and that of their loved ones. The skills were also impor-tant when the slaves were manumitted, or when they es-caped, or after the Civil War. And then, because we are talking about the children of African and European parents, all this — the skills in a craft and in European ways, the chance to get free, freedom itself — all this was conflated with light skin. And because over the generations, as the men in the slave master's family had sex with the slaves with dark skin, and then with slaves with lighter skin, the offspring of these unions became even lighter. So it was not very long before widespread sexual contact between Africans and Eu-ropeans, and the rule of hypodescent, combined to create a group of free blacks and slaves and former slaves with very light skin — black people with green eyes and red hair, or blue eyes and light brown skin, or brown eyes and straight hair.

Some of this group, when freed, moved to cities, where

their light skin and cultural attributes—language, education, skills—made possible the creation of a light-skinned black elite. And because light skin then, as now, was the most important marker of status in this country, many of this group came to use light skin as an independent mark of status. Historians also tell us that dark-skinned blacks who had other attributes of high status—a skill, a formal education, wealth— were often excluded from the social life of these elite communities because of their dark skin.

In the early years of slavery, there was some tendency for white Americans to see light-skinned African Americans— whether slave or free—as a separate group with a distinct political and social status that lay somewhere between the status afforded the black and white groups. This was especially true in South Carolina and Louisiana, where the legal system formalized this tripartite scheme of racial classification. This tendency ended, however, by the middle of the nineteenth century, as pressure on the South with respect to slavery caused it to intensify its control over the entire slave community. During this period, then, there was less tolerance of manumission, and less tolerance of any other special treatment for slaves with light skin. At the same time, the "one-drop rule" gained even more support nationwide as it helped defend the notion that Africans were "natural slaves." Thus, as the white community began to withdraw privileges from the light-skinned black community in the mid-nineteenth century, the light-skinned group started to seek out alliances with darker blacks. This new sense of unity accelerated during the Civil War and Reconstruction and was solidified during the Jim Crow era and the Black Pride movement of the 1960s.

The history that surrounds issues of race and color is, of course, much more complicated and interesting than is suggested in this brief introduction, which is almost misleading in its brevity. But there is a sense in which, even if this brief historical sketch shades into stereotype, it is the story that most black Americans know about race and color. And it is a history that scars us all. Just as the forced migration of millions of Yoruba and Ibo wrought destruction on those cultures in Africa as well as in America, so has this newly created African American community been devastated by a vision of the world in which light skin and dark skin are seen as meditations on good and evil, civilization and savagery, intelligence and ignorance. This cruel lesson has not only affected how we see ourselves in comparison with white Americans; it has also informed how we look at each other within our own community.

Because black and white Americans talk and write about race so much, I can say, with some assurance, that at any given time many blacks hate, fear, and despise white Americans, and that many whites hate, fear, and despise black Americans. And even though black Americans rarely talk or write about the color distinctions we make within our own community, I also think it safe to say that, at any given time, many light-skinned black Americans and dark-skinned black Americans despise, are attracted to, fear, reject, and are rejected by each other simply because of the color of their skin.

And it was into this America that I was born, in the fall of 1940.

Like my parents, I am a black American with white skin, an African American with both African and European ancestors. Thus, I live a life that is often disjointed, troubling. I also see the world in a different way. There is something about living on the margins of race that gives me a unique view of the categories "black" and "white," that presents a different picture of white Americans and black Americans, of America itself. For my position does not allow me the luxury of thinking that the notion of race makes any sense. If you are black and white at the same time, once you finally realize that it is not *you* that is strange, you realize that something very strange is going on in this society. Perhaps more directly and more starkly than other Americans, I understand "race" as a socially created metaphor, for my very existence unsettles expectations of "race." It is no longer a tangible reality as reflected through color. Indeed, my existence raises troubling questions. Suppose race really *does* have nothing to do with color? What, then, is it all about?

Calling the categories themselves into question troubles people. But I did not write these essays to cause trouble. I wrote to make sense of my life.

The first section of the book starts with notes I wrote in a journal in 1979 as I began to grapple with these old, old issues of identity. Some ten years later, these notes became the basis for an essay that described my life as a white black woman, described what it is like to be both inside and outside the black community and the white community. In that essay, "Commonalities," I also showed how I have been able to find similarities between my life and the lives of others, thus finding a community I call "home."

The publication of this essay freed me to write more about race and color in America. The essays in this book describe that exploration. In the first cluster of essays, I use stories from my life to explore various topics, including how race and color intertwine through black and white families and across generations; how members of both black and white communities work to control group membership; and what happens to relations between black men and women when the layer of color is placed over the already difficult layer of race. I describe how white black Americans long for and assert kinship with other black Americans, and I explore the survivor guilt that holds sway in many of our lives. I also address how one can tell — and *whether* one can tell, who is indeed "black."

In the last essay in this group, "The Re-Vision of Marginality," I move from exploring the problematic nature of being a white black woman, to examine the positive aspects of this doubled identity. I describe this new understanding of my position as one of being bilingual and bicultural. Thus transformed, being a white black American is not merely a troublesome quality; it is also a gift that encourages me to partake of the treasures of two cultures, thereby helping me to be open to many, many more.

The next cluster of three essays focuses more directly on issues of race alone. The first, "Affirmative Action and Stigma," speaks of my struggle with racism as a black professor at a white university. My struggle is probably similar to that of other black professors. But that is an important point here. For it is important to know that white black Americans are still black, and that once white Americans understand that you are black, they construct your racial identity the way they always do — by treating you badly because of your race.

Because questions of creating and maintaining racial identity lead directly to the question "What do we really mean by 'race'?," the next two essays address this question. In "Skinwalkers, Race, and Geography," I try to apprehend the concept of race by comparing racial boundaries with geographic boundaries. In this process, I discover that exploring the overt task of drawing geographic borders helps explain the covert task of drawing racial lines. In "Where're Your People From?" I try to grasp the notion of race by contrasting it with the concept of ethnicity.

The final essay, "An Ordinary Day," replaces America's dream of racial purity with a dream of community. And this dream — that we can all live together as brothers and sisters — is one that sometimes comes true, if only for a few moments, an hour, a day. This is the story of one such day, a day I spent in a small nearby town, at the invitation of one of my students — Michael Campbell, a member of the Iroquois Cayuga tribe, Turtle Clan. Through his generosity, I was reminded once again what a gift it can be to be brought into the community of another. This day was a present from the Campbell family to me. Sharing it is our gift to you.

I want to mention just two more things. The first is the power of silence, because although Americans talk a good deal about race, there is an enormous and weighty silence that surrounds the issues addressed in these essays — problems of color, and the longing for racial purity. As we begin opening these topics for discussion, we might need to address this silence too. Why does it exist? How is it maintained? And whose interests does this silence serve?

Finally, I want to address the issue of the very limited resources available to the black community. There is no doubt that we already have too many difficult problems confronting us: bad schools, bad housing, no jobs, and drugs. The question might well be raised: "Why do you want to add yet another issue? We've got to put our resources where it really matters!" And here is my answer: I am not suggesting that we not expend all our resources fighting the oppression of black Americans in all its forms. I am only suggesting that, at the same time, we try — all of us — to be more kind to one another. This does not take time, energy, or money. It only takes wanting to do it. It might be possible to heal some of the wounds within our community. And if so, it can only make us stronger.

Commonalities: On Being Black and White, Different, and the Same

Many in my family are various shades of brown, as is common in most black families. Many others of us, however, look white. I wrote these journal notes, and this essay, as a way of coming to terms with the dilemma of being black and looking white in a society that does not handle anomalies very well.

Only recently did I realize that the work I do is deeply connected with my struggle to live within this dilemma. I am a lawyer and a professor of law. I write about the intersection of race and sex in American law, focusing on the status of black women in the law — that is, on the group that stands at the intersection of the race category and the sex category. I used to define my work in that way. Now that I have written this essay, I see my work differently. In this essay, I struggle to combine two statuses that our society says cannot be combined: black cannot be white, and white cannot be black. In my earlier work on race and sex, I argued that it did not make sense to try to maintain two distinct categories of race and sex in the law when that separation ignored the very real existence of black women. There again I argued that the categories seen as so pure were not pure, that the boundaries thought impermeable were not impermeable. Looking at all of my work, I now understand that I have been working at the intersection of race and sex because I exist at the intersection of race and color, and because I understand, in a very profound way, that in order for me to exist I must transgress boundaries.

I think this makes people profoundly uncomfortable. Categories make the world appear understandable and safe. Nonetheless, in this essay I ask you to experience my vision of the world—a world where the categories do not clarify, but only confuse, a world where one must question the very existence of those categories in order to survive.

Journal Entries: November 1978–December 1981

November 1978

He sang out:

> What did I do
> to be so black and blue?

And I wept:

> What did I do
> to be so black,
> so white?

November 26, 1978

I wish I had a name to make my home in, to hide inside of. Maybe we should bring back the name "mulatto." For a woman, the French would say "mulâtresse." An identity. A group to belong to. You say "mulatto," and it conjures up meaning: a person despised by dark-skinned brothers and sisters.

("Who does she think she is? She think she white, man."
"Hey, you think you better than me, huh?!")

Cast out, cast out, always cast out from the only home, the only safe place, the only refuge in a terrifying, vicious land. Cast out, and alone.
No home. No home.
No place to belong.
No place to rest a frightened and lonely heart.
No place to hide.
White people would let me in, of course. They think that I belong with them. They smile at me. They welcome me. They think I'm their sister.

("Did you see the way that nigger drives? We shouldn't give them licenses!")

They think I'm on their team. And so I'm always waiting, waiting for them to say it. Please don't say it. Don't do that to me. Jesus God, cabbie, can't I even go across town in a cab without having my whole identity called into question? Always wary. Always fighting their silent thoughts, their safe assumptions. Fighting for control of who I am.
That's who I am. Cast out of my house.
And fighting for control.
And crying.
Missing the safe warmth of my childhood, a colored girl growing up in the protection of a strong family in the segregated South, surrounded by their love and their strength and their definition of me and of themselves.
We moved to New York City when I was very young. One of my warmest memories is of traveling back to North Carolina from New York every summer on the Jim Crow train. We children belonged to all the black adults on the train. Everyone talked and shared food: fried chicken and white

bread, pimiento cheese sandwiches, deviled eggs — our shoe-box lunch.

Yes, I can see that. What I'm missing is the protection of the family.

But I lost something more when I grew up and moved out of the segregated South, out of the safety of my childhood home, because the Jim Crow laws gave me an identity and a protection I couldn't give myself.

Suddenly, the world was opened to me: streets, movies, schools, restaurants. I put one foot into the world of white-Jewish-liberal-intellectuals when I was in the fifth grade, and I've been straddling two worlds ever since.

What do you do if you're rejected by one world,

> ("Oh, let's have Judy sit at the table with the white couple when they get here. She acts so white.")

and are constantly rejecting the other? I am perceived by some as white, by some as black, by yet others as a black person but "really white," so (a) you can trust her and (b) you can't trust her.

And yet I'm me all the time.

Jerked back and forth by other people's needs and fears 'til it gets hard for me to figure out who I am in all this.

I'm glad I've started this writing.

These are the notes of a white black woman.

> ("Mommy, which water fountain should I drink out of, white or colored?")

December 1, 1979
Sometimes I feel like I'm black, passing for white.
Sometimes I feel like I'm white, passing for black.
On a good day, I just live my life.

December 2, 1979
I went to hear a chamber music recital last night at the Kennedy Center. This is the kind of music that filled my child-

hood—chamber music at the WQXR studio, symphony music at Tanglewood or Lewisohn Stadium, the Saturday afternoon opera on the radio when we were not allowed to make a sound in the apartment.

White music.

We were also exposed to black music—spirituals, "boogie-woogie," and the "classical" black composers and musicians. But our father disapproved of the rhythm-and-blues records we brought home when we were teenagers. As an adult, I have spent a long time getting in touch with other kinds of black music. Bill introduced me to jazz. And I was almost thirty when I first heard the blues. I couldn't get over it then, and I still can't. It speaks so directly to me and for me. It pierces my heart with pain or joy, sometimes both. And gospel music I have loved since I was a child. I loved it when the men's choir at St. Catherine's AME Zion Church went on summer vacation and took their tacky cantatas with them. For that's when the gospel choir came. And the church jumped and shook, and the music made you feel.

It is hard, but very important, to fit the black and white music pieces comfortably into who I am. I need to be able to accept the black and the white heritage with their own validity.

That is all true, and important, but getting a little too intellectual. A way of avoiding the anxiety of last night's chamber recital. For you see, color makes it all more complicated. The concert hall seats maybe eight hundred, a thousand, people. It was almost full. And I didn't see anyone who was not white. I felt very anxious and frightened. I was losing control of my identity as a black person. It was slipping away. Wasn't this proof that I was white? By their perception, didn't I fit in just perfectly? And wasn't it obvious that I wouldn't have been there if I weren't white? (1. All people who go to hear chamber music are white. 2. I go to chamber music recitals. 3. Therefore, I am white.) But at intermission, I saw about half a dozen black people. The pendulum tilted back to center and I was steadied.

I must gain better control over who I am. I must learn to live squarely, steadily, and surely in the middle of ambiguity, centered strongly in my own No-Name. I must define the No-Name and make it my home.

December 15, 1979

More and more, lately, I have been thinking of dating white men. I have been thinking I could now date white men. I just returned from a visit at Julie's house. One of their friends stopped by. I was attracted by his looks, his openness and enthusiasm, his excitement in learning. Sexy.

I think it would be difficult. But with some help, I could do my part. I think this means something good in terms of my defining and accepting who I am, a white black woman. My definition of who I am is much less at risk.

And it also feels sad, terribly sad. For I am, after all, a black woman, deep down where it counts, and where it hurts.

December 19, 1979

I remember having a startling thought several months ago. Someone gave me a standard line about how she had always wished she were tall. I started my standard response of how I wished I were short—when I suddenly realized that just wasn't true. I liked being tall and looking good tall.

Then last week I saw "Death and the King's Horsemen," a play by the Nigerian playwright Wole Soyinka. I was watching the beautiful dark-skinned women dancing and started my standard thought of how I wished my skin were that color. But that thought was immediately replaced by "That's not true. I like the way I look. I look just fine."

I was startled. Pleased.

Hopeful that the thought will return.

There is so much yet I have to tell you about.

About the silence, the lifelong silence of my family. Was it such a terrible secret that we dare not talk about it? What was the secret? And what would happen if we did reveal it?

And about the guilt of a survivor, always protected by a white-skin disguise.

   Is it a disguise?
   How am I to take the good things that come my way?
      Would that cabbie have stopped if he had known?
      Would the doctor be civil if— ?
      Would the clerk have been so helpful?
      Would the real estate agent have rented me the apartment?

How can I say "No, don't be nice to me. I'm black?"
How can I try to keep from passing when all I'm trying to do is catch a fucking cab?
There is no way around it. I am passing all the time as I walk through the world. I can only correct the perceptions of those persons I deal with on a more than casual basis. And I feel like a fraud. And I hate it. I hate myself for not being able to solve the dilemma. And I hate black people and white people for putting me out there.

Catching a cab is just as hard for a white black person as for a black black person.
Or maybe not.
Maybe it has to be made hard to punish myself for my clever disguise.

I heap ashes on my head and beg for forgiveness.
Sackcloth and ashes.
If I am forgiven,
perhaps I will be allowed back into the fold.
Will someone forgive me?

January 24, 1981

I am beginning to understand what they have done to us. The anger. All the anger we can't show. And all of the men depressed. And the women, abandoned, uncherished, un-beautiful—

What will become of us? How can we save ourselves and each other? How do we raise the children? How do we protect the children? (Another body found in Atlanta today.) Tell me, how do I raise a black-man child? Why am I raising a free child who knows what he is feeling? Maybe black men need to be depressed to stay alive. Feelings released create energy and potency. What can a black man do with those?

I am free to feel my aliveness, to stretch as far as I can— because I'm a woman, because I look white. Today, as Pat was getting off the elevator, a white man grabbed her and pushed her back, saying, "No nigger is going to get off this elevator before *me*!" I am spared that craziness by looking white. I am not pushed, abused, humiliated on a daily basis. I have my own craziness from being white/black, but I am not damaged the same way. I get to meet the test of what is called "beautiful" because I look white.

And so I can be valued as a woman by black men. Because I am not so damaged by the racism that I hate them. Because, coming from a white/black family, my father was allowed to make a good living and give us so much—financial security, protection, an open door to the world. Because I can feel beautiful.

It is, I think, the ultimate betrayal, the ultimate irony. The crazy way that racism worked has allowed me to be free and potent. And it has kept the men I love locked in. And impotent. They are enraged at me for being able to take such joy in life and to feel the strength of being whole.

I feel enormous guilt at my whole-ness, at feeling potent, at my joy in life. Luckily, there is a built-in price I will have to pay. Being alone. I can't go back to being less than I am. I want to stand on my toes and reach my arms up as high as I can. But I haven't yet found a black man who can stand watching me do that.

I weep for their need.
But I weep for me also.

". . . some dreams
hang in the air like smoke
touching everything."

PLENIPOTENTIARY
And the world said: "Yes.
You may have everything.
But you will have to be alone."
"Well then,
suppose I have a little less.
Suppose my mind doesn't work so well,
and my body too . . .
then may I have someone?"
The answer is still out.

December 14, 1981

Oddly enough, the last chapter is the hardest to write — not
because it is painful, but because there is no demon driving
me. I am writing now not as part of the learning, the exor-
cism, but writing to record what I have learned.

As I have moved into adulthood this year, as I have come to
a strong sense of my own self-worth, I have learned to make
my home within myself. My definition of who I am is steady,
and is not shaken by the definition of others. I do not have
to cut myself or stretch myself into one procrustean bed or
another. I am content to be who I am, and leave to others
the comfort of their own definitions. I claim only myself, and
define myself by my own name.

This does not mean that there is not, will never be, confusion
or pain at being a white black woman. What it means is that
it does not control me. It cannot claim me. It is a dilemma I

live within. I center myself in myself, in the ambiguity of myself, and move on with life.

> ¡Soy bi-lingüe, bi-cultural,
> y orgulloso de mi raza!

The bright, bold poster says it for me:

> I am bilingual, bicultural,
> and proud of my people!

There have been signposts this year which marked the journey. I remember reading the blatherings of a newspaper columnist who argued that his dark skin entitled him to a special position as spokesperson for black people. I remember being stunned, as I reread *Black Rage* this year, at the authors' angry description of "fair-skinned dilettantes" who take out their self-hatred on those with darker skins. What I remember most is that it was immediately clear to me that the authors were not saying anything about me, but were saying worlds about themselves. And I remember the day I made a joke about the color of my skin. It was a *good* joke — free and cloudless! My friend and I laughed and felt good together.

And I have learned from good teachers this year. I remember especially Pauli Murray's autobiography, *Proud Shoes*, where she tells of her struggle to accept her white slaveholder ancestors as part of her family, where she tells of her struggle to accept herself. And Joel Williamson's book *New People: Mulattoes and Miscegenation* — what a revelation. If there is a whole book on the unspeakable, it can't be taboo, but an issue capable of exploration and comprehension. Williamson described the history of a new group that has been created through the fusion of Africans and Europeans. He gave me a history, a context. He saw me, and validated my new sense of being.

And I have learned from the poetry of Chinese women and Native American women — women who felt the anguish of

losing their unique ethnic identity and who were determined
not to lose it all, determined to fuse the two worlds through
their poetry. A determination to be all one is, and for that
"all" to be more and more, and not less and less. I will travel
with Zora Neale Hurston, who has taught me with her life
and who said: "But I am not tragically colored . . . No, I do
not weep at the world—I am too busy sharpening my oyster
knife."

There is a phantom pain. It comes and goes. It will always
come and go. But the pull toward selfhood, toward wholeness, is stronger. By being, I fuse the two worlds. I need do
no more.

———◆———

There she stood in her pink organdy dress,

    pink socks,
    pink ribbons,
    patent leather shoes.

She had rich brown skin
Hair pulled back in braids so tight

    bright eyes
    bright smile.

She was me when I was six
getting ready for church on Sunday morning—
organdy dress so starched
it scratched,
head tender from the curling iron
Mommie wielded so fiercely:
pressed hair for Jesus, Lord!

    pink ribbons,
    pink socks,
    patent leather shoes.

So I smiled at her,
seeing myself.

And she hid behind her mother's legs
looked up at me
and said

"I'm skeered of white people."

Reflections: July 1989

This is how the exploration started, with notes in a journal.
It was time for exploring old wounds, a time for growth. I
was newly divorced, a single-parent head-of-household. And
newly come to the world of therapy. It was a time for working on unfinished business. It was a time of rapid, often
forced learning. I had been pushed out of one world—not a
happy one, but a known one, and therefore a safe one. And
this must have pressed on the bruise of aloneness, of feeling
pushed out and homeless because of being a white black
woman.

I say unwanted, "forced learning," but clearly it was
learning that I wanted, because I went out looking for it. It
was a time when I began to open up to the world in a new
way, and began to be able to see all the resources and gifts
the world made available to me. I began to see that although
perhaps I did not see on the table the food that I wanted,
there was enough on the table for me not to starve. And, as
time went on, I began to see that indeed there was a feast on
the table, and that it only took opening up to the feast,
reaching out to the richness of life.

It was about this time that I began to hear echoes of my
song in the songs of others, that I began to realize I was not
out in the world, a stranger and alone.

It was then that I began to see the many similarities between my feelings of sadness and strangeness and what
others felt. How then could I be so sad when I was so much
less alone. I was finally able to hear the stories and songs of
my sisters, and I heard them say:

We are like you.
You are our sister.
We are with you.
You are not alone.
We feel the same pain.
We sing the same songs.

Let me tell you who spoke to me, and what I heard. Let me tell you how they answered my call. Let me tell you how we are the same in our differences.

Listen to the song of my Indian sister Janet Campbell:

DESMET, IDAHO, MARCH 1969
        At my father's wake
            The old people
            Knew me,
            Though I
            Knew them not,
        And spoke to me
        In our tribe's
        Ancient tongue,
        Ignoring
        The fact
        That I
        Don't speak
        The language,
        And so,
        I listened
        As if I understood
        What it was all about,
        And,
        Oh,
        How it
        Stirred me
        To hear again
        That strange,

Softly
Flowing
Native tongue,
So
Familiar to
My childhood ear.

How this song moved me! I heard then, and hear now, a deep and moving love for her people, a profound memory from childhood of belonging and being safe in the embrace of her family and her people. But I also hear a sadness at the not-belonging-anymore. The loss of her father, the loss of her language, the loss of her home.

I remember summers spent with our grandparents, aunts, uncles, and cousins in North Carolina. We played all day long, as we roamed from family home to family home, enjoying the freedom from the city streets, enjoying the sunshine. We ran through the grape arbor quickly, in hopes the bees would not be able to catch us. We wriggled our bare feet in the grass as we played "Simon Says" until it was too dark to see anymore. And then the wonderful dusky evenings, when we sat on the front porch with our mother and grandparents, swinging and fanning, trying to keep cool. Sometimes my grandmother would let me water the petunias in the urns on the front steps (Did they like that night watering?). But most of all, I remember it as a quiet, coming-together time. And I remember, like Janet Campbell, the murmurings of the grown-ups as they talked about whatever they talked about. I don't remember what they said. But I do remember the dark and quiet stealing over us all on the porch, enveloping us in quiet and safety. And I remember being embraced and comforted by their murmurings, sounds that lulled us to quiet and to rest.

Now I return to the South to visit my parents. And once again, as I go with them into the black Southern community—the church, the bridge club meetings, the college convocation—I am transported back to my childhood, to the safe embrace of family and community and church.

(''Lord, child, I can sure see your Aunt Estelle in your face. I would know you anywhere!'')

''And, Oh, How it Stir[s] me To hear again That strange, Softly Flowing Native tongue So Familiar to My childhood ear.'' And yet, and yet, I too have left home. And I hear the sounds of the language, but I am no longer of the language. One day, in church with my parents, I wept from the beauty and from sadness. Because although I was reminded of coming to church as a child, when I was safe in the embrace of my family, my church, my community, and my God, it was an embrace that I now returned to only rarely, and then as an outsider. It was a borrowed embrace. And I wept at the loss of leaving home.

This is, of course, a loss all of us know. And we all try to recapture or re-create that embrace as best we know how as we grow older and leave home. But there is something about moving from the southern black community to the northern white community that adds to the sense of loss, of homelessness.

It makes me think of a story I heard about Dr. M., a resident in psychiatry. When I first met her, I felt her warmth and kindness. I noticed her quiet competence, and her quite visible pregnancy! I saw her as a woman filled with life. When I mentioned her to a friend who was also a psychiatrist, he said, almost in passing, that he had not realized she was an Indian until one evening when they were both on duty at the emergency psychiatric clinic of a local hospital. At that time, an elderly Indian man was brought in for emergency treatment. I don't think he said why the man was there. What struck him was Dr. M.'s statement that this man had left the reservation, and that reservation Indians are particularly cruel to those who leave the reservation. I was immediately stunned by the thought that Dr. M. was talking not only about this man but about herself. Had she also "left the reservation"? She was clearly successful in a white world. How much had she paid for that success? And it was clear also that she was talking about me. For there are so many reservations: geographical ones, cultural ones, and reservations of the mind. When one leaves to explore, to live in another world, are you leaving the reservation? How do those who don't leave the reservation feel? Do they want to leave? Are they afraid to move into a hostile world? Are they mad because the world off the reservation is more welcoming to me, a white black person? There is no doubt that the members of the white community in my northern home are more welcoming to me than the members of the black community. How painful that has been. And I can't tell if it is because I am so bilingual and bicultural that they are not clear that I am black, or because I have left the reservation and must be made to pay for it. But I am clear that I miss the sweet language of my childhood. And I miss my home. My Indian sisters have helped me see that more clearly.

And there was yet another poem that, years ago, led me to see my sameness in my difference. Listen to the song of my Chinese sister, Laureen Mar:

CHINATOWN I
SEATTLE, WASHINGTON
She boards the bus at Chinatown,
holding the brown paper shopping bag
with twine handles that comes from
San Francisco or Vancouver.
It is worn thin with creases.
An oil spot darkens one side
where juice dripped from warm
roast duck, another shopping trip.
Today there is fresh bok choy
wrapped in Chinese newspapers.
Grasping the rail with her right hand

she climbs the steps carefully,
smiling at the driver, looking down
to check her footing, glancing
at him again. She sways down the aisle
as if she still carried wood buckets
on a bamboo pole through the village,
from the well to her house.
Her gray silk pajamas are loose,
better than "pantsuits."
Sometimes there are two or three women,
chattering with the quick, sharp tongue
of the wren: dried mushrooms too
expensive, thirteen dollars a pound now.
She sits down and sets the bag between her knees.
Her shoulder is close to mine.
I want to touch it, tell her I can understand
Chinese. Instead, I stare at the silver
bar crossing her back, and hope she knows
this is an Express; it does not stop before Genesee.

What do you see when you read this poem? I see the generations of Chinese women stretching back, from the old woman climbing the bus steps so carefully, to her mother, who "carried wood buckets on a bamboo pole through the village, from the well to her house." But has the line of Chinese women stopped? The writer knows she is a Chinese woman. She knows Chinese. She wants to touch the old woman, to let her know that she knows Chinese, that she is family. But she is prudent. She does not do so. But tell me, if others do not know you "know Chinese," if others do not know that you are family—are you family? Are you Chinese? Who controls what is real? Can you do it yourself, or do you need the corroboration of others? The writer wants to reach out, to help, to belong, but dares not. She is and is not family. She is the same and not the same.

It reminds me of the girl in the pink organdy dress. I *knew* I was like her. I remembered being her. And I reached out with a smile. But she saw only the white part. And it frightened her. Her fear said, "No, you aren't *my* family. Go away." She didn't know that I "knew Chinese."

But my Chinese sister knows my song and helps me see that I am not alone.

It is not all mournful work. Some of the lessons I have learned have been through rowdy laughter. I have had funny teachers. Let me tell you about Dianna. We worked at the appellate division together. And one of the strange things about that office is that it was comprised of about twenty attorneys all in various stages of avoiding writing a brief. One day, when I was in the "walk-the-hall" stage of avoidance, I dropped into Dianna's office and started complaining about the general run of men about town, and the general level of confusion and poverty in my life. "What I need," I said to her, "is to find a prosperous, slightly boring dentist to settle down with." "Oh, I know just what you mean," she declared emphatically. "And if you find one, ask him if he has a sister!" We burst out laughing. And that's how I learned that Dianna was a lesbian.

It wasn't until years later that I realized that, like me, gay people are faced with the problem of "coming out" to people. Dianna has to decide when she should come out to someone, and how. She has to worry about how that person will respond. And as long as she keeps meeting new people, she will have to keep dealing with those issues of self-identification and exposure. These are issues I deal with also. When do I tell someone that I am black? And how? And how will they respond? And if I don't tell people (the apartment rental agent, the cab driver), aren't I "passing"? But Lord knows there's no reason for me to get into self-revelation with someone who's paid to drive me from home to the car shop.

"And why?" I think. "Why should my lesbian sisters have to come out to people? Why are they not allowed to keep their sexual life private? Why do they have to say: 'This is who I am. I hope you can deal with it. Even if you can't, I need for you to know who I am. I am a member of a despised group. If we are to know each other, you must know this.'" As I write the words, I know why they must come out. They must be clear about who they are, and one way to do this is to force other people to see who they are. As I do. This is also why I "come out." And, with them, I brace myself for the flinch, the startled look, the anxious intake of breath, the wary eye. I come out to white people to say to them: "Beware. I am Other. Proceed with caution." And I come out to black people — how painful it is to have to do it, to say "I am family. You are safe with me. I am you." But, of course, if you have to *say* that you are black, if your skin doesn't say it for you, then how safe are you, really? How can you be family? And again, I brace myself not so much for the startled look (black people are used to white black people) but for the wary eye. For I am still Other. Coming out only proclaims how I am different, not that I am the same.

I think sometimes how similar are the problems my lesbian sisters and I pose when we come out. Does the person who hears me come out have to confront the notion of black being white? Does the person who hears my lesbian sister come out have to confront the notion of female being male (that is, if one who loves women is a male)? How unsettling it must be to have someone announce to you that black is white, that female is male. We are talking about "transgressed boundaries, potent fusions, and dangerous possibilities."

My lesbian sisters have shown me that I am not the only one who has to struggle with coming out. Their courage gives me courage.

The last story I want to tell you is one that I am really not proud of. I like to think it would not have happened if we hadn't been so tired and jet-lagged. But we were. There were eighteen of us coming from all parts of the country for a two-day board meeting in Oakland. We were a group of feminist lawyers and activists, a group very self-consciously created to represent as many different kinds of women as possible. In general, we enjoyed getting together enough to travel thousands of miles for a grueling two-day session. It was a group of women who are smart, considerate, funny, and committed to women's issues. Our first meeting was scheduled for Friday night at eight o'clock. We decided to hold the meeting at a restaurant near the hotel.

Now, you must remember that for some of us, meeting at eight in the evening was in reality meeting at eleven in the evening, after an exhausting day of travel. Nonetheless, we were all energized by being together, and off we went to search for a restaurant with a table large enough to accommodate us. What a relief it was to find one, only a few blocks away. There were about a dozen of us, and we were seated around a large round table. Menus came out along with pots of tea and cups for sipping tea. We started to relax, to look with relish at the menu, to talk about what we would order and how we would share the food. And it was then that Dai broke into the overtired, energetic talking and said with a flat voice, "I think we should all consider leaving this restaurant." Dai travels through the world in a wheelchair. And it appeared that this restaurant *was* wheelchair-accessible, but only if you didn't mind going through the back door, past bags of smelly garbage, and through a dirty corridor. Dai was visibly wounded by that process, and although she was by now seated at the table with us, she thought we should leave in protest. There was a long silence. And I don't remember exactly what happened next. But what I do remember is that, at first, no one wanted to leave. There was the suggestion that perhaps we could go ahead and eat, and write a letter of complaint to the management later. Dai was bitter, and angry at us. "You wouldn't stay here if there were an entrance for blacks only." I remember being torn by her analogy. Was she right? But surely not. The only reason she couldn't come in the front door was because she couldn't maneuver her wheelchair up the stairs—a physical, not political, problem. Not a problem of status and degradation. But what I remember most clearly was being angry at her for having to deal with her anger when all I wanted to do was to enjoy my all-too-late dinner after an all-too-long day.

Eventually, of course, we left the restaurant. Two of the group stayed behind to explain to the manager why we left. Another was given the task of writing the owner about his noncompliance with relevant regulations on accessibility. We decided to check the restaurant for compliance before including it in our material for conference attendees that spring. But what struck me the most was that instant when I recalled a conversation with another black woman academic returning from a conference composed predominantly of white feminists, one of whom stated that she was tired of dealing with the anger of black women. We were outraged by their "fatigue." But that evening in Oakland, I saw that I could be—no, *was*—like those white women who were tired of dealing with my anger. For I did not want to deal with Dai's anger. And because I was not in the wheelchair, I was the one who was empowered. I was the one who could listen or not, pay attention to her anger or not, understand or refuse to understand, let my hunger for my own comfort get in the way of recognizing her pain. Dai showed me that in some ways, and to some people, anybody who is not in a wheelchair, be they black, Chinese, Indian, gay, is the insider. And she is the outsider, beating on the door, crying for inclusion. Wanting to be seen, wanting to be known.

I have learned many things from my sisters about being different and being the same. Sometimes, like that time, I did not want to learn the lesson. But it was an important lesson. I learned that sometimes I am the one who gets to wave "the magic wand . . . of exclusion and inclusion." I am like Dai, who feels her difference and her exclusion so keenly. But I am also the nondisabled one. And thus, I am the insider. I am like my white sister too.

There are many more stories I could tell, for once I was able to see the commonalities I see them everywhere. And yet there are more questions, so many more unanswered questions.

I have been wondering why difference is so hard to accept. I have been wondering why difference makes us all so anxious that we create categories, and then expend enormous amounts of energy to make sure people fit in them, and stay in them. And I have been wondering why the system of dualism is so important. What is there about a continuum that is unsatisfying? Frightening? Why must life — and we — be seen in either "black" or "white," with no shades in between? For it is this system of rigid dualism that fosters so much anxiety when people don't fit into the categories neatly, when people "transgress boundaries."

And why is it that we look so hard for sameness when we are, each and every one of us, so different from each other?

And why is it that we find it so hard to find sameness, when we are, in so many ways, so much the same?

But this is work for another time. For now, it must suffice that I have come a little way along this path. I have been engaged in my own struggle with being different, and I have found, along the way, the sameness, the connectedness, I needed. I have been able to see the commonalities, and have found a home.

Afterword and Preface

It is of no small moment to break a lifelong silence. I did not do so easily.

The first step was a small one: I would put words on paper. But writing the words in a journal was itself hard, for writing the words meant that it was true—true that I was a white black woman, true that that fact dislocated my life, and hurt. In order to put those words on paper, I would have to acknowledge that pain and its power in my life. I wrote to face it head-on. Ten years later, I took these journal excerpts out of a drawer, pushed by a need to rethink, develop, amplify—a need to visit this place once more. It was much like the need to return to the scene of an ancient trauma. We go back in order to go there as a visitor, a visitor who can come and go as she chooses. We go back to remind ourselves that that place holds less terror, that we have left it behind, that we have moved on.

"Time, the prophet of wisdom."

The decision to publish came later. And that decision was less about publishing than it was about finding a way to speak about the unspeakable. It was the telling that mattered. I needed a way to break the silence. It felt dangerous. Why did no one else talk about this? What would happen to me if I did? Why risk the saying? But could the saying be any worse than the not-saying, the hiding, the pretending that there was no pain? Perhaps I would have made a different decision had I been able to have conversations in secret with others — if, for example, others had written poems or stories about their life as a white black person. I could have whispered my story to them as they confided in me. But I found no such stories or poems, and we do not speak of such things in the black community. We make fun of others, we shun others because of their color, but that only means that we move the pain outside of ourselves and put it onto someone else. We do not do the hard work about color, perhaps because so much else is so difficult for us.

I would have to publish in order to force the beginning of a conversation. But how could I even think of saying something so private to strangers, to publishers, if I could still not say these things to one person? How could I begin the beginning?

I gave myself a way to proceed. Cautiously. I would force myself to show "Commonalities" to twenty people. I would speak the unspeakable to twenty. Then, and only then, would I allow myself to send it out to publishers. I would wait as long as it took.

It took more than six months. I sent a first copy out by mail. I dropped another into a mail chute in a front door. I asked for comments, and I waited. Anxious. Fearful. What would they think? Would they punish me for talking about these issues? Would they be aghast at finally knowing who I was? Would they be polite and distant? Silent?

Time went by. I sat at the dining room table and stared at the unopened envelope addressed to me. What had my reader seen? What had she said? Did I have magical powers that could change rejecting words into accepting ones before I opened the envelope? Long minutes passed.

I need not have feared. I had chosen my readers wisely. They were not aghast or distant. They did not reject the person they were now seeing from a different angle. They said: "I did not know. . . ." They said: "I was moved. . . ." One called from the airport: "Yes!" And they gave me the courage to speak to more, then to more, and to yet more.

"Commonalities" was published as a law review article in 1990. Almost immediately I began to receive letters and telephone calls from other white black people—American and Canadian, men and women, from teenagers to the elderly, people I knew and people I had never met. This is what they wrote:

> "I guess it should come as no revelation to you or me that so much of what you say has a special meaning and resonance for me. God, I have thought so many of the same thoughts and had so much of the same pain. . . . I don't know whether to laugh or cry about how much I wanted to fit in and belong somewhere."

> "Thank you for your article and for putting into words so many things I have felt, half thought, and never found the means to express."

> "I've felt that way too sometimes. . . ."

> "I can't believe that happened to you too. I thought I was the *only one in the whole world* that felt like that about myself. How did you have the courage to even think about writing this stuff for others to see into your head? My God, how I appreciate the fact that *you did it!*"

> "I've been astounded by how many insights and perceptions we share on the matter of race and racial

identity, and how similar our experiences have been in certain ways."

"Thank you for the article. It really helped me to bring up some of those awful feelings about looking white and being black."

"I often find myself pained at the realization that the definition of blackness is not nearly wide enough to encompass how I look. I am not recognizable to other black people as black, and am amazed at how alienated my confluence of genes can make me feel. . . . All of this does not make me completely comfortable about the possibility that I am somehow denying what I am, and am somehow complicit in a society that has created a permanent black underclass. Anyway, this is rather long-winded, but the chance to respond to an article on a topic on which I have agonized, seemingly in isolation, for so long, without acknowledgment that other people could be living something similar, was important to me."

They showed me that my experience of the world was not a singular one, but a shared cultural experience.

Many other readers also taught me. They saw commonalities I had not seen, and told me their story. I learned that black people who do not look white can also feel homeless, caught somewhere between black and white—the dark-skinned child raised in a white community; the brown child with one parent who is black, one who is white:

> . . . I guess it isn't all their fault
> how could they really know
> that two halves of their separate worlds
> still can't make me whole. . . .

Other black people of various shades and hues told me of their own pain around issues of color. We started to talk about how cruel we are to one another in the black community about this matter. We started to talk about what we could not talk about before.

I learned more. I learned that Jews with blond hair also have to "come out," that they too watch carefully for incorrect, treacherous assumptions when they go to Germany, my America. I learned that bisexuals, rejected by gays and straights alike, feel homeless. So do those who are labeled different or eccentric. Some told me of other boundaries they had transgressed. Another recognized that I was revisiting an old pain in order to undo its power, and used my visit to do the same. By opening the door to a hard issue in my life, I opened the door for others.

I had thought the writing was the important part. It was nothing compared with the sharing. Finally speaking words that I had been afraid to speak was a step away from weakness, a step toward my own sense of power. I had thought I was "out" before. I wasn't. Not like this. I have discovered in new ways that these socially constructed wounds hurt most where there is fear and secrecy and shame. I understand better than ever my connection to my gay and lesbian brothers and sisters.

I had thought the writing was the important part. It was nothing compared with what I have gained from breaking my silence.

"Write more," they said. I was pleased, yet surprised. Wasn't it finished? But indeed, I had more to say about color and race in America. I have learned to trust what my readers tell me. I am learning to trust my own voice. I write these essays with a sense of relief and release.

I have been silent too long.

The Lesson

Place: An elegant reception in New York City

Time: Some time in the fifties

The white man was astonished, perplexed.

He stared at the tall, distinguished-looking man standing next to him. A man clearly of some substance. A man with white skin, straight hair, aquiline nose.

"But how can you tell that you're a Negro?" he asked innocently, stupidly.

And my father answered:

"Because America tells me so."

Stories We Tell

One of my favorite family stories is about Aunt Midge — not really my aunt, but my father's. The youngest sister of my father's mother, Aunt Midge is only ten years older than my father. Perhaps as a result of being the baby of the family, Aunt Midge always seemed playful to me. When I think of her, I see her laughing, her eyes twinkling. My father always seemed to brighten up when Aunt Midge was around. They would go off together into another room and tell bawdy stories. Those are the stories we children didn't get to hear.

But this is a story about Aunt Midge that I did get to hear. It took place in Charlotte, North Carolina, her home town. And it must have been very soon after the buses in Charlotte were desegregated, perhaps sometime in the 1950s.

She was riding on a bus. In my mind I see her as I always remember her. She is short, an apple-dumpling-plump, grand-motherly-looking woman with delicate, translucent skin, rosy cheeks, and fine white hair waved around her face. Would she have been wearing a flower-print dress and carrying a large pocketbook? Had she been shopping? Did she have a shopping bag? I think so. That's how I see her, late in the afternoon on a hot, tired day in Charlotte.

The bus was almost full, a few seats here and there, black and white scattered throughout the bus. And then, at one stop, a dark-skinned black woman got on, looked for a seat, and went over and sat down next to a white woman. And this is why I think the buses hadn't been desegregated for very long — because this white woman was outraged. How *dare* this colored woman come and sit down next to her without so much as a by-your-leave! The white woman noisily gathered up all her bags and packages, rolled her eyes, muttered under her breath, and flounced over to sit next to Aunt Midge — Aunt Midge, a black woman with porcelain skin and baby blue eyes. She settled in with a haughty glance at the other bus riders, a glance that said: "No, *indeed!* Some people may be willing to sit next to niggers, but *I* am not one of them." The other black riders, friends and neighbors of my aunt, tried to suppress a grin. But then Aunt Midge peered around this white woman and her packages, and smiled and waved at them, and they couldn't contain themselves any more. They exploded with laughter. They laughed until the tears rolled down their cheeks. They laughed until they had to hold their sides. They laughed until they were out of breath. "Lord, Lord, white folks sure can be a fool, can't they!" And I guess we have to say, "Yes, they sure can."

Another story I tell is about the principal of a high school in New Jersey where I taught French in the early 1960s. Although my husband and I lived in New York City, where he was a graduate student, I was teaching in the suburbs because the selection process for city teachers appeared unending. So my first year of teaching I commuted from the Upper West Side in New York City to a small town in New Jersey. It was a long trip. There was the 6:15 A.M. walk to the sub-

way, the 6:30 subway ride to the George Washington Bridge
bus terminal, the 7:15 bus ride across the bridge and into
town, and the twenty-minute walk from the bus terminal to
the high school, where I arrived just in time for the 8:30 bell.
By the second year, we decided it made more sense for us to
live in the suburbs and for Bill to commute to New York
City for his classes several times a week. We would have to
find an apartment in northern New Jersey.

I already knew this would not be easy. It had been so difficult to find an apartment in Manhattan that we eventually
filed a complaint with the city's Human Rights Commission
against the owner of one apartment building. I remember
that the hearing was held during the summer when I was
teaching in Ohio and that Bill drove all the way back to New
York to participate in the hearing. When he returned, he told
me the apartment-building owner had died of a heart attack
soon after he got the summons, and that at the hearing his
wife had screamed it was all our fault. And I remember being glad he had died. All this was in my mind as we started
to look for an apartment in northern New Jersey in 1963.

It was, of course, as bad as we had expected. Everything
that was "available" over the phone was "already rented"
when we arrived and the owners saw us. They probably
thought we were an interracial couple, but that was bad
enough. One day, in the faculty lounge, I told a few colleagues we were having a hard time finding a place to stay
because we were black—did they know of anything available in the area? It did not take long for the word to spread.
I was called into the principal's office the next day. He
looked uncomfortable. Did he hem and haw? Probably not.
He was a former Marine and probably went straight to the
point. "Mrs. Ellis, I have just found out that you are a Negro. I am worried that something might happen in the
school, some kind of disruption or violence. So I thought I
would make an announcement over the P.A. system and let
everyone know that you are Negro. Just to avoid trouble.
You understand." I was stunned by his fear and his seeming

irrationality. Nonetheless, I calmly explained that it was very unlikely that anything untoward would take place in a French class, but that if anything inappropriate were said, I had years of experience handling such comments. He seemed relieved. I left the office. No P.A. announcement was made. But let me tell you, I have told this story plenty of times to my black brothers and sisters. And we roar with laughter as we imagine what the P.A. announcement would have been: "Nigger alert! Nigger alert! We've been invaded! Man your stations!"

White folks sure can be a fool sometimes.

Black people tell these stories all the time. We laugh at the ignorance of white people. But it is a laugh with layers of bitterness and rage. We laugh instead of striking out. We also laugh as a way of showing our superiority, for we understand many things that white people do not understand. Laughter and mockery are two of the powers of the weak. But I think that white black people tell these stories for an additional reason. We tell them as a way of stating allegiance, of claiming kinship. We tell them in order to remind our darker brothers and sisters that we too know what white people are really like. We know it in a different way and have special knowledge to share. We are in the family too.

So don't forget, white folks: we see you, we hear you, and we tell our stories. Was that you at a party joking about living in "Coon City"? Little did you know that one of those "coons" was at the party and is writing about you even now. Was it you at a bar talking about that "new nigger basketball player at the university," not knowing that the "nigger basketball player" was two chairs away? And when you were in surgery performing a brain shunt and said it was hard to cut through the skull of your patient because "Negro skulls are so thick," you never knew that the brilliant new resident you were working with was a "Negro."

We tell our stories.

And we are everywhere, white folks.

Beware.

Family Pictures

When Big Buddy died, my mother and her sisters met at the funeral for their only brother and decided we should start having family reunions — "Or else," they said, "pretty soon we'll just be getting together at funerals." For our first reunion, we went back to Winston-Salem, North Carolina, where they were born and raised and where we children were born and spent our childhood summers. Several years later, my cousin Barbara hosted the second reunion at her home in Montgomery, Alabama.

The first picture in my scrapbook of that weekend is one of my mother and her two sisters, my aunts Gwen and Willa Mae. I smile at the picture even as I write these words — three sisters, happy to be together on a blue summer's day. In the picture, my mother is standing on the left, wearing a long flowered dress she made. My aunt Gwennie is in the middle, with her arms around her sisters. These sisters have always been close. Even now, they call and visit each other. They share the good news and the bad, up and down the East Coast.

In the photograph, my aunt Gwen is wearing a subdued, pastel dress, as befits the wife of a minister. I always loved being at their home those summers in Winston. I remember Gwen ironing and cleaning and cooking as she listened to "As the World Turns," and I remember my uncle Crawford in his study preparing Sunday's sermon. I liked going to Mount Pleasant to hear him preach. How proud I was that my uncle was the preacher! Sometimes they invited me to go with them to Crawford's mother's home for Sunday dinner. Her dining room was cool and dark. I can see her now, sitting at the head of the table with a gentle smile. Sometimes she asked me to go to the backyard and pick mint for our iced tea. How special I felt then. And how I loved being in that family. This is where I wanted to stay at summer's end, when it was time to pack our steamer trunk and travel back to Harlem.

I smile too as I look at my aunt Willa Mae. She is standing on the right in a bright orange and yellow dress, long to the ground. That dress epitomizes how I think of her—bright and bold and daring. When I was a child, I thought she and my uncle Alphonse were quite exotic. In their home on Long Island they had serapes and hats from trips to Latin America. Just imagine—they had been to another country! And when we went to their home for Christmas or Thanksgiving there would be foreign students Alphonse had invited to join the family celebration. They also had a backyard with a hammock and a fish pond full of large goldfish, all of which was quite amazing to a child who lived in an apartment in Harlem. What was most exciting of all, however, was our once-a-year outings with them to the beach at Far Rockaway. This was always quite an excursion. We first took the subway to their home on Long Island, then piled into their car for the ride to the beach. What remarkable relatives these were, who could take us so easily to another world—a world of picnics on the beach and dashing in and out of the water, and the wonderful crashing noise of the waves.

My uncle Big Buddy had died, of course, before this reunion, so he is not in any of these pictures, and really, his picture in my memory is quite vague. But what I remember is a jovial, heavy-set man who liked to take us children around with him as he went about town. And what wonderful places those were! We accompanied him to his bail-bond office, where he let us rummage through his desk drawers until we found paper and pencils for our "work." He let us go to the pool hall next to his office to see what was going on, and to get bottles of pop from the ice-filled chest on the floor. I also remember tagging along with him once on a trip to a dimly-lit juke joint, an exciting but probably unauthorized outing.

So these are the pictures I am seeing of my mother and her sisters and brother at the Scales Family Reunion. And then I turn the page in the scrapbook and see a picture of all of their grandchildren who came to the reunion, grandchildren whom they forced to sit still long enough for a group picture. Quite frankly, these are gorgeous children. There are twelve of them — my son, my nieces and nephews, my cousins' children. They range in age from eighteen months to twenty-two years old. Many of them were meeting for the first time. They were enjoying their newly found cousins, and delighted in running in a pack. The older cousins took charge, and simply announced to us when they were taking off with the younger ones. The younger were, of course, delighted to be out with the "big kids." I'm not sure exactly what they did, although I think it included seeing movies they weren't supposed to see, acting rowdy in the theater, eating junky food, and staying up way too late. In the photograph, they are all sitting on the back steps of Barbara's house, the older ones with their arms around the littlest ones. These children are well loved.

It seems a shame to change the lens on the pictures I am describing for you. I do not want to disrespect my family or the memories of that reunion. But I must tell you about the color change that took place in my family within the two-generation period from my mother's generation to my son's generation.

When you look at the photograph of my mother and her sisters, you see that two of the women have white skin. So did my uncle, Big Buddy. But then, when you turn the page to look at the photograph of the grandchildren, it almost takes your breath away, for these are all brown-skinned children. Their skin color ranges from light brown to dark brown, but it is clear that these are not white children.

I don't remember anyone ever talking about color in my family when I was growing up. I certainly never heard anyone urge us to pick dark-skinned spouses so our children would not be mistaken for white. And the color change over two generations could be the merest coincidence — and not even a remarkable one at that, since most black people do have brown skin. But it does make me stop and wonder to what extent the question of color entered into our choice of a spouse.

I had thought that somewhere in these essays I would be writing about the anxiety I used to feel about being attractive to the dark-skinned men I dated. Why were they attracted to me? Was it because of who I was, or was it mainly because of the color of my skin? As Lorna C. Hill has written:

> I want to lay in the arms of a black
> man who loves me because I am beautiful . . .
> Not the next best thing to a white woman . . .

This is how I felt. This is what I thought. And I am just now realizing that I was so anxious about how they viewed my color that I did not consider the value I attached to theirs. For it is very likely that without any instruction, without conscious plan, without even thinking about it, I — and perhaps others in my family—thought seriously about skin color when I thought about who would be the father of my children. For this is a country where it is dangerous to be too dark, and where it is wrong to be too light. And we try to protect our children.

Africa in My Hair

I recently talked with a graduate student about her research: she is studying women's perceptions of their bodies. She told me she has noticed that white women write about their weight but black women always write about their hair. And so shall I. I can tell my life story through my hair.

The story of my hair is the story of trying to control wildness. When I was a child, my hair was long, thick, wild, out of control. How I longed for the wavy hair of my older sister, the curly ringlets of the younger, or the straight hair of my parents. My mother used the techniques all black mothers use—braids, barrettes, ribbons, curling iron, hot comb. She asked the hairdresser to thin it out; she used a soft brush for those short frizzy edges around my face, and a hard brush for the rest. I have strong childhood memories of sitting on the floor every morning while she struggled with my hair. And I remember how she fixed it: two long braids

in the back, with one in the front. In the summer the braids
were rolled into buns and pinned in place with prickly bobby
pins. And on special days the hot irons came out and I was
given long, fat ringlets, with ribbons to match my dress.

The problem became more serious when I became a teenager and looks became so important, for looking beautiful
meant looking white, and looking white meant straight hair.
Every minute I was in the house my hair was in curlers,
curlers that would change the wildness into carefully controlled curls for a little while. Even then, the curls lasted only
as long as the air was dry. Oh humidity, oh rain, how I
feared you and despised you! No showers, no swimming, no
sweat! Chemical straighteners came on the market my last
year in high school. How marvelous that was—no more
wild hair, no more terror of the rain. When a friend told me
one day that I looked like a model from *Seventeen* magazine,
I was delighted. Finally I had straight hair to match my light
skin. Finally I looked beautiful. Finally, I really looked
white.

All of us black girls showed up at college panicked about
our hair. Those who had their hair straightened with a
straightening iron wondered where they could get their hair
done in that small college town, while I wondered if my hair
would grow out so fast that those nappy edges would return
before I could get my hair straightened again during the holidays.

I don't remember why I stopped straightening my hair after college. I controlled the wildness by wearing it pulled
back in a French twist or a bun. Perhaps I wanted to look
more mature, more sophisticated than I felt: I was a new
teacher and a new bride.

How wonderful it was when the Black Power movement
came in the '60s, and we could stop worrying about our
hair: hair was free, and so were we! We cut our hair short
and wore it "natural." Our older relatives were in shock,
and we were in rapture. It was the first time my nappy hair
and style were on speaking terms. It was a time when I not

only made peace with my hair, I exulted in its thickness and wildness. It was a wonderful time.

But that time was short-lived. For now, as I get older, my hair gets thinner and straighter. It is also turning gray. Oddly enough, the gray is not so problematic, for although it signifies a loss of youth and of beauty, although it suggests a dignity and power that are contrary to ideals of female attractiveness, this was an expected loss. It is the second loss, the unexpected loss, that is so deeply felt: I am losing the mark of my African heritage. For although I wear Europe on my face, I wear Africa in my hair.

White people, as usual, never understand. When they look at my hair, they see Italy or the Middle East. But when black people see my hair, they know. They see Africa. And those who don't "know" at least wonder. And I didn't know how content I had become with my share of Africa until now, when I am threatened with its loss.

I think God must be laughing—not a mean laugh, but a chuckle, as she shakes her head from side to side: "Unh, unh, unh! There's just no pleasing some people!" After years of struggling to straighten my hair, now that age is straightening it for me, I look in the mirror and despair. On those dry, wintry days when the cold air sucks the moisture out of everything, I long for the humidity I once feared. The same woman who once did everything possible to avoid moisture now exults in a steamy shower. And she waits impatiently for warm summer days when the air is moist once again, and her hair returns to its old African ways.

(Laughter Helps!)

I know it was meant as a compliment, but by the time I heard the same comment for the third time in a week, I just lost it. It was, once again, about hair. Three times that week (*three times!*), different white women had stopped me on the street to tell me how nice my hair looked and to ask where I had gotten my "perm." These were, of course, words that were meant kindly. And there's nothing wrong with asking for advice. But the women were also saying that they understood me to be a white woman just like them who had gone to a beauty parlor to have this beautiful African texture put into my straight hair. The first two times, I was polite to these absolute strangers. I thanked them, told them the "curl" was natural. But by the third time, I had had it with not-quite-true politeness, and the truth just pushed its way out: "This is not a permanent. This is just the way my hair is. And you can't get it from a beauty parlor. You have to be born colored and wait forty years for nappy hair to come into style."

I was still simmering later that day when I went to the beauty salon near my office for a haircut. So I told this story to Alice, the young white woman who trimmed my hair every month. And she jumped up and down with glee: "Oh no, Judy, don't tell them that! Tell them *I* gave you the perm! Send the business to me!"

Shock and Fear in America

Frankly, I am one of the most boring people I know. I teach school, pay my parking fines on time, stop for schoolbuses, and walk my dog three times a day. I spend holidays with my family, enjoy reading to little children, and love cooking for friends. My idea of a great summer vacation is to stay here in Buffalo and go to baseball games, cookouts, street fairs, outdoor concerts, and the pool. Like you, I worry about cholesterol, getting older, inflation, and elderly relatives. I don't smoke, get dizzy from one glass of wine, and am generally asleep by 10:00 P.M. So it is quite astonishing to me, then, when I am seen as an object of shock and fear. Here are two stories to show you what I mean.

The first incident took place some time back, when my hair was thick and curly—true African hair! I had gone into a drugstore to buy—I have no idea what. All I remember is standing at the checkout counter, where the clerk was look-

ing down, glancing back and forth from the items I was buying to the cash register. When he got the final tally, he
looked up to tell me how much I owed. And that's when his
mouth dropped open and his eyes got big and round. He was
shocked. "What happened to your hair?" he said, aghast.
(Reader, this was not a Bad Hair Day!) I told him *nothing*
was wrong with my hair, that this was just how the hair of
black Americans looked. My guess is that he had seen my
white hands on the counter and expected to see straight hair
that would match. He was not finding the match. And it
shocked, frightened, him. But he had a way to address his
fear: "You should go and get something to put on your hair
that will straighten it. That way, people will think you are
white." By then, I was speechless. I paid for my goods and
left the store. (To this day, I don't remember what drugstore
it was or what city I was in. All I remember is the man's
comments, and that he was an East Indian. And I think of
this incident whenever I meet an East Indian. Thus is preju-
dice born.)

The second incident took place just last year right here in
Buffalo. I had met a friend for lunch at a restaurant, where
we had a good time talking and laughing and eating good
food. After lunch, as we got up to go pay our bill, a middle-
aged white woman came over and asked me where I was
from. Thinking we might have met before, I said "Washington, D.C., New York City, North Caro—." But she inter-
rupted me: "No, not that. I mean where did your family
come to America from?" I replied, "Africa and Europe." She
shook her head—still not good enough. "No, no. What
country in Europe?" Still patient and smiling after such a
nice visit with my friend, I tried to answer her question once
again: "I really don't know." By now, she was almost beside
herself. "What do you mean? How can you not know?" So I
told her: "Because the slave owners did not keep genealogi-
cal records on their slaves and then distribute them to the
slaves before they escaped or were freed." And that's when
she hit me. Now, it wasn't a punch or anything like that. It

was just a slap on the arm, delivered with a tight smile and a "now you *know* that's not what I meant!" It was the kind of thing you might do to a friend, to say, "Oh, you're just teasing me!" But I didn't know this woman from Adam, and she was definitely angry. I was not giving her the right answer, I was saying things she didn't want to hear. Well, it turns out that she had friends in Germany, and she thought I might be related to someone she knew there. But as we were finally leaving the restaurant, my friend said: "Good heavens! Does this happen to you often?" And I answered, wearily, "Yes."

I see these two incidents as similar because both times, while I was just going along minding my own business, leading my quiet, humdrum life, I apparently inspired shock, fear, anger. These two people got upset because there was not a good fit between what they saw and heard, and what they expected to see and hear. This disjuncture upset them and they wanted me to do something — straighten my hair, pretend Africa did not exist, pretend the enslavement of Africans never took place — to make them feel better. They were Procrustes, and I, the unwitting traveler who must be stretched or cut to fit his one true and perfect bed.

A friend once called these stories bizarre. And, I wondered, does he think my life is "bizarre"? Does he think *I* am "bizarre"? So I thought I would set the record straight: I am, quite frankly, a pretty regular person. I cry at sappy movies and enjoy a good joke. I love deep-dish pizza and Rocky Road ice cream. If you saw me on the street, you would never give me a second glance. It is not I who is bizarre. What is bizarre is the power of the fiction that there are two racial categories, black and white, that these categories are discrete, and that the borders of these categories are inviolable. What is bizarre is the power of the belief that history and biology will somehow conform to the social rules of this country. And what is bizarre is how much we are all like Procrustes, who would not let reality intrude on his dreams or his longing or his fears.

Choosing Up Sides

"Whatever he does, he had better not bring home a white girlfriend!" she exclaimed. We laughed. There were three of us, black women friends who had gotten together after a long absence, talking about our lives, our work, our men, and, of course, our children. Her son was not yet a teenager and would not be bringing anyone home for quite a while, but she was already clear about his choices.

I laughed too, but I sensed a vague discomfort at her words. It took me awhile to understand that feeling. But I finally understood that I was uneasy because she had rejected part of me, the white part, with her statement. And I was uncomfortable—fearful that my disguise might not hold, fearful that she might suddenly "see" that I was a white black woman. Michelle Cliff says it well: "She who was part-them felt on trembling ground." I also finally recognized that my laughter was dishonest: why laugh at my own rejection? But I did laugh. I laughed because, at that moment, my hunger to belong to that group of friends was stronger than my ability to be true to myself.

I thought about this for days. And what kept returning to my mind during that period were thoughts of Grandpa Tate, my father's maternal grandfather and the only white blood relative I ever heard of. I know little enough about him. I know that he was born sometime in the 1860s, and that he was a barber. I know that he married my great-grandmother Mary in 1886. I think he loved and respected her: I have a silver-plated dish inscribed "1886–1911" that he gave her on the occasion of their twenty-fifth anniversary. I know he made enough money investing in real estate to raise ten children in comfort and send them off to college. I have a picture of Grandpa Tate with his wife and children, taken around 1905. They all look healthy and well-dressed and well-groomed. It is clear that Grandpa Tate took good care of them. I know he was white, of Scottish origins. I also know that his wife, and therefore all of his children, were black. I think of the contribution Grandpa Tate made to my family, to me, and I am not willing to reject him. I respect and honor his memory and claim him as a cherished relative.

Racism is so deeply embedded in our consciousness that we don't often realize that society asks us, on a regular basis, to reject part of our family when we are required to take sides in this tragic war-game of race and color.

> "Which side are you on, black or white?
> There is a war going on.
> Allegiance must be clear.
> Choose!"

But choosing up sides means buying into the craziness of American-style racism. For there are many black Americans with white ancestors, and there are plenty of white Americans with black family members.

This is the way the American system works: if you have one parent or ancestor with African origins, you are black.

You are not a member of the white family that might also claim you. That family must renounce you, and you must renounce it. You are in the black family, as will be all of your children and your grandchildren and your great-grand-children. It is by thus redefining "family" to exclude their black family members that white Americans keep themselves and their "family" white. The notion of "family" in white America has very controlled borders: "family" stops where "black" begins.

The result is, then, that white people are all "white," and that black people are a wide range of colors — white, rosy, olive, tan, brown, reddish, black. We are forced to choose up sides, but the American rules dictate that choice. Real facts, like who your parents and grandparents were, don't matter: only social facts count.

Several years ago, a strange and sad incident took place at the law school. It involved a moot-court program sponsored by a national association of black law students. A young woman at the school who wanted to participate decided to join the local chapter of the association. But it was not as easy to join as she had expected, for although her father was black and she had African features, her mother was Puerto Rican. There was furious debate by the students in that chapter as to whether she could — or should — participate in a program for black students. Finally, they arrived at a solution. If she would renounce her Puerto Rican mother, she could join the association.

I hope this sounds as sick to you as it does to me. Renounce her mother? Were they all mad? And yet is this not what we all require of ourselves, of our children? We do it all the time. We renounce the reality of our real families, and we embrace the unreal reality of a social construct.

Think about it for a minute: whom have you renounced today? and why?

Are we all mad?

There are two little girls whom I love. They are two years old. The world is theirs to explore, and they go at it full tilt.

Anyone old enough to read these words would be hard-pressed to keep up with either of them for an afternoon. These little girls are sisters in the deepest sense of the word, for they are twins and have been together from their earliest watery memories. They speak their own language and giggle at their own secrets. But they are twins who do not look alike. One is brown, like her father; the other is fair, like her mother.

I once talked about the problems color would present them with their father, a nephew. And I wondered, would they too be forced to choose up sides? How would they choose? Whom would they renounce? How could they? And why should they be forced into such a cruel dilemma? Their father's family is from Africa and Scotland and other lands; their mother's family is from Scotland and other European lands. It is just as misleading to say that they are African American as it is to say that they are Scottish American, for their heritage is complicated and rich. And I wonder sadly if there is any chance that these little girls will ever be able to just be Americans.

Think about it, for it does not involve my family alone. It involves yours too. And we really should do better by our children.

Let me be clear. I am not claiming that I always see these complications. I often think and speak as if the categories "black" and "white" are real. I am just as hungry for a place to belong as anyone else. I am just as willing as others to choose up sides. But living on the margin forces me to live with, and therefore to see, the complications. And it is very complicated indeed. For the truth is that all Americans with some African ancestry are indeed "black," because that is how we are defined, and that is how white people treat us, and that is how we are raised. But the truth also is that "black" people are not *only* "black," since we also have ancestors who came from Europe and Asia and South America and the South Pacific; we have ancestors who were Cherokee, Choctaw, Lumbee.

I am torn by my understanding of both truths, which exist side by side at the same time, for it means that we both can and cannot choose up sides. It is holding both these truths in my hand at the same time that is so difficult — and so important — to do.

"Mo' Black"

One of the delightful things about living in academia and learning the language of that "country" is that you get to make fun of it in its own language. Take, for example, the simple act of burping. Well, once scholars get hold of it, once we decide to study it, the burp is no longer simple. This is how it could look to the legal scholar: "Bodies and the Law: Deconstructing the Post-Modern Burp." The mathematician might write: "Essential Discontinuities, or Functions That Burp." And the sociologist might present a paper entitled "A Cross-Cultural Analysis of Burps in Eastern European Immigrants to New York City, 1900–1910." See what I mean? Really, you just have to laugh!

And one of the wonderful things about being black in academia is that because you speak both black and white you get to poke fun in two languages. So it was with yelps of delight and hoots of recognition that I listened while Anna, a light-skinned black professor, described her "Mo' Black Theory of Adaptation."

"I tried going back to Africa," she said, "but, girl, I spent an hour explaining to this African about how we are black too — a separate lost colony within this already lost colony — and he never would believe it." I reminded her it was in France that James Baldwin understood for the first time that he was indeed American. She said "Yes! There was this brother running around the university telling us we all had to go back to Africa. And I said, 'Hey, I have *been* there. Ain't no welcome for us there.' And this guy, would you believe it, he's even lighter than I am! What was he trying to prove? Trying to prove that he was 'mo' black' than anyone else. He must have been 'mo' black,' 'cause he was the baddest-talking brother around. And if you listened to him, maybe, just maybe, you wouldn't notice the color of his skin."

"And what about our great black leaders?" she continued. "Malcolm and Du Bois and Walter White — and how about Angela? Just how dark were they? And didn't they do wonderful things for our people? Oh, I'm just sick of it. Why do we have to feel so guilty all the time about how we look? Why do we have to keep being 'mo' black,' trying to make up for all the wrongs we have done? I haven't done *anything* wrong. I was just born looking like this."

She was mad. A good, healthy mad, I thought. I liked her anger, her honesty. I liked seeing that she had been thinking about this for a long time. And I agreed with her. You know, people can hand you a plate full of guilt, but you don't have to eat it. Push it away. Eat something *good*.

I thought some more about our heroes and heroines. And I wondered how much of their work was tied up in their need to expiate the sin of colorlessness. Malcolm X was harassed a lot for being light when he was young. Darker black kids called him "snowflake" and "milky." He was also the lightest-skinned child in his family: some of his brothers and sisters called him a "freak of nature." Anna continued: "You know, Du Bois was obsessed with dark skin — "

Most of the lawyers I know are civil rights lawyers. I am always startled when people describe lawyers as sleazy crooks, con artists, because these are not the people I know. The lawyers I know are hardworking, passionate people, committed to social justice, both hopeful and distressed about the possibility that their work might make lives better. Most of my other friends and acquaintances are involved in social change — as teachers, writers, civil rights activists, government workers in civil rights agencies. And the truth is that many of these people are black people with light skin. Some are often mistaken for white. I have no way of knowing whether a disproportionate number of light-skinned black people are in these jobs. Certainly, the field is disproportionately black in general, both because of our interest and because so many other fields are closed to us. But I wonder if any of them, like I, went into the civil rights field, in some measure, as a means of expiating our sin — the sin of how we look.

But although we try to atone as a way of escaping the rage of our darker brothers and sisters, that doesn't mean that we do escape. ("No," she said, "I would *never* hire a light-skinned attorney in this office. Our clients just wouldn't stand for it!") We are easy prey for the weak and the vulnerable. We are available, right there in the office, in the neighborhood. And we are powerless too. Beating up on us is the "next best thing" to beating up on white folks.

One incident comes to mind. I was at a social gathering, one of those events where everyone is dressed up and on their best behavior. A group of professionals, black and white. Some of them I knew, others were strangers. Halfway through the evening I started to talk with a black man with dark skin. We had mutual friends. We also discovered that we had both grown up in Harlem at about the same time. "Where did you live?" he asked. I gave him the address.

"Oh," he responded, "you lived on Sugar Hill, up there with the rich folks, up in the fancy part of Harlem." (An unsmiling smile. A sneer?) "I was raised at the bottom of the hill, on the other side of the park. The poor side." "Well," I answered, "I guess you win." He was thrown off, confused. "Win what?" "I guess you win the 'who-suffered-most contest,'" I said. I dropped the line, dropped the subject, and moved on to talk with someone else.

Yes, you're right. That was a mean thing to say. And maybe some of you don't know what was going on in that conversation. But I have been in that kind of exchange so many times I have finally figured out how to handle it. He pushed the middle-class-kid-with-light-skin guilt button: how high would I jump? I was supposed to feel awkward, confused, embarrassed, guilty at my good fortune. He also pushed the "mo' black" button — for the more deprived your childhood, the "mo' black" you be! I answered his sneaky meanness with open meanness, and I guess I don't get points for that. But let me tell you, it felt good to push that guilt away. I didn't want it. It felt good to say, "I know that game, and I'm not playing. I know my lines and I won't say them. Sorry, buddy. Work out your own stuff by yourself."

It's not that I don't know that color and class are connected in this country. White people, like all of us, are less frightened of people who look like they do. The degree of difference marks the degree of acceptance, and thus the degree of entitlement to food and shelter. But surely no one would suggest that I not feed my family because of my uncertainty about why I got a certain job. I do not carry as much guilt or craziness or integrity as the philosopher Simone Weil, who, as a Jew in France during World War II, ate only the amount of food given to Jews in Nazi concentration camps, and starved herself to death. I understand the guilt of a survivor. I accept my share. But frankly, enough is enough.

So, no, I am not going to apologize for the fact that my parents were able to provide me with a secure childhood, a childhood where I never wanted for food or clothing or shelter. It is only what every child should have. And no, I am not going to apologize for the fact that I was born with light skin. Every mother's child should be able to look in the mirror and smile back at how she looks. Don't even think of passing me that plateful of guilt any more. Life has better things for me to eat.

Definitions

It happened again just last week. I was at a dessert party with some old friends — old friends and friends of theirs whom I was meeting for the first time. All white. While talking with one of the men, the topic turned to civil rights issues. Even more treacherous, the topic turned to affirmative action. In an attempt to warn him that racist comments would be inappropriate, in an attempt to avoid having to leave the party after such comments, I let him know that I was black. But clearly he had been forewarned, because he was not surprised. He was, indeed, ready. And he replied, with a smile: "No, you're not."

I am used to this denial. If I look like you, and if you are comfortable talking with me, then I cannot be Other. Sometimes it is said in shock, dismay: "No! You can't be!" Sometimes, in confusion: "But you don't *look* black." Sometimes, like this time, it is said calmly, with a certainty that the speaker, not I, controlled my identity. I was polite but firm: "You are wrong. I am black. You probably just don't know what black people look like." He did not press further. But I was stunned, as I am so often stunned by the sense of entitlement to define that so many white people have. He was clear that it was *he* who would tell me who I was: I would not name myself.

Sometimes my authority over the question is given some weight, even if the listener is incredulous. And the question is asked often even if you don't hear it. Do you know that those government bureaucrats you talk to are checking little boxes marked "black" or "white" during your conversation? Assume it. They do. In a society based on racial stratification, the state must keep track of who is who. I always assume also that the race-namers will get it wrong. I correct them. Often they are embarrassed. They mutter "Oh," avert their eyes, correct the form. But sometimes they get a real attitude.

I remember one time in particular, after the cab I was in crashed into the car in front, then backed into the one behind. A policeman stopped to help. He took down the story. As he was taking down my name and address, I noticed that he had checked the "white" box. "Officer," I said politely, "you made an error on your form. I am not white. I am black." He gave me a long, bored look, decided not to discuss it, and said, "Sure, lady. If you say so." If I say so? If *I* say so! As if it were my idea! I was enraged at his assumption that all of this—the categories, the racial purity laws, the lives that are stomped, mangled, ruined because of those categories and those laws—was based on my say-so. If *I* said so, we would do away with all of it—the sickness and fear, the need to classify as a way to control, the need to make some appear smaller so that others can appear larger. "If I say so" indeed. No, you cannot give that to me. I am not the one who "said so." You are, Mr. White Cop. It is all smoke and mirrors, but it's your smoke, your mirrors. I am willing to go by the rules to the extent that these rules gave me a home, for I intend to keep my home. But you don't get the chance to construct and reconstruct my reality any way you choose every twenty minutes. That decision was made some fifty years ago when I was born, when the state required that my parents indicate my race for the birth certificate. They obeyed the state's laws of racial purity and wrote, quite correctly, "colored." And so I am. Like you, I have a piece of paper that tells me where I belong in the state's system of racial hierarchy.

An Indian friend once explained to me about the piece of paper that Indians must obtain if they want to be called Indians. Because the state wants to know who is Mohawk, who is Cherokee, who is Lakota, it requires that tribes enroll those whom they accept as Indians. Tribes have the authority to "enroll" whomever they choose. And because who is enrolled often says who gets to participate in the political life of the community, the decision as to who gets that piece of paper — that is, who gets enrolled, who is an Indian — takes on a political cast, as with all racial purity laws. My friend was able to get a piece of paper that showed she was enrolled: she was indeed an Indian.

So here is the good news about America's racial purity laws, on the reservation and off. If you don't wear the yellow star of degradation on your face, the state has a piece of paper that will mark it for you. Like the king of Denmark out for his morning ride, the star of David emblazoned on his armband, I wear my yellow star with pride. Like him, I wear it to show solidarity: "Come after my brothers and sisters, come after me." The difference is that the king's star was borrowed: he was not really Jewish. But my star is truly mine, and no one may take it from me.

Sometimes, I must admit, the silliness of this racial-definition business gets to me. It is all smoke and mirrors, a lawyer's trick. But at the same time, it is profoundly serious, because so many fall for the trick. It sometimes strikes me funny, at other times, deadly. Sometimes I am enraged that white people can live in this country for so long and be so ignorant of how the racial purity laws work. It is, of course, the ultimate privilege, this not knowing. And then sometimes, in very much the same situation, when I explain to a white person that I am black, when they immediately accept it as meaningful truth and modify their behavior accordingly, I am amused by their ignorance, by their ability to believe such a silly thing, that white is really black. I am amused by my ability to trick people. "What a fool this person is," I think. The system is, quite frankly, ludicrous.

It reminds me of a conversation in the book *Drylongso*, a book of interviews between the black anthropologist John Gwaltney and residents of black communities around the United States. Gwaltney is blind—a fact he considers an asset to his work, for people feel they should obey the injunction to help "the sick and afflicted." His blindness was an important element in his interview with Clinton Banks, a sixty-year-old "street man." At one point in their discussion of race and color, Gwaltney pointed out that anthropologists consider Indians from the country of India "white," Caucasian. There was a pause, and then Mr. Banks said, "Lawd! Lawd! I think that is rotten of them to lie to a blind man like that!" I laughed when I read that. Now there is a man who knows make-believe when he sees it! Just saying that the emperor is wearing clothes does not make it true.

Or does it?

It is like the idea of money. What a complicated notion that is—junk bonds, leveraged buyouts, basket trading, upside volume, futures-related index arbitrage. This mysterious language intimidated me until the day I realized that this entire structure is based on a pile of rocks (isn't gold a rock?). It is based on who has the most rocks (isn't the one with the most gold the richest?). And it is based on who has the prettiest rocks (isn't 14-karat gold worth more than 10-karat gold?). It makes me think of little boys crouched on the sidewalk swapping marbles. Who will get the most? Who gets the big aggie? We read articles in *National Geographic* about tribal peoples who use feathers and beads as a medium of exchange. We say, "How charming! How primitive!" And we never stop to think that putting all your rocks into a pile and counting them, trying to get more rocks than Billy, is not a spectacularly sophisticated activity. Like the matter of race, it only works if you believe.

If you believe that having a lot of pretty rocks means you may have food and shelter, it will be true. Only believe that people can be sorted out by "race," and that that sorting has meaning, and that too will be true. Tinkerbell will live, if you just believe. And, fools that we are, we do.

———◆———

Strange as it seems to think of being fair in discussions of race and color, it would be unfair *not* to say that other black people try as hard as white people to take my yellow star away. They see themselves as tribal elders, able to grant or deny tribal membership at their whim. They will enroll me, or they won't. It must be intoxicating, exhilarating, to arrogate this power to exclude, especially if one has so little power to begin with. The black student who received a poor grade in my course used his small power like a rapier:

> Frankly, I don't understand why you thought you hired a black professor when you hired Prof. Scales-Trent. She looks white to me.

I was relieved to see it in print—an old ghost companion taking on body. "Oreo!" we cry out, hurling the word at each other like a javelin. "Apple!" the Indians yell, in a running attack. "Banana!" snarl Asian Americans, snapping at their brothers and sisters with sharp teeth. Who can hate us the way we hate ourselves? Who can hurt us the way we hurt each other? We define one another out of the family, then run back to our lair, still snarling and fighting, and lick our wounds, alone.

"WILL THE REAL BLACK WOMAN PLEASE STAND UP?" asks Audre Lorde.
Who is the "real" anything?
Who is left?

Marion and Effi

"Girl, you are just not going to believe this! Have you got a minute? I know, you just got back from work. But trust me, this is good! Did you get this week's *Jet*? No? Well, listen to this headline, right on the front cover: 'EFFI BARRY reveals: Mayor Wanted Her Skin Darkened To Protect His Image As A Black Man.' Can you believe it? What do you mean, 'darken how'? With a sunlamp, how else? Now listen. This is what happened. It turns out that the first time Marion Barry ran for mayor of D.C. folks were talking all about how his wife was 'too light.' You know how we do! Yeah, you're right. White folks probably didn't like it either! It says here Barry told her to go get a suntan. And he went out and bought her a sunlamp. Well, that didn't work. She was still 'too light.' So he sent her to a resort, Hilton Head—you know, in South Carolina?—to soak up the sun and get herself a little color so she wouldn't appear too light in the pictures. Now, I'm not real surprised that he married Effi. Marion just likes light women. Look at Rasheeda! But, you know, Marion is a stone politician. And if it's going to hurt him with the voters, Effi will just have to look more black. 'Be light, but not too light. Look white, but not really' — man, talk about a trick bag! No, I'm not surprised that he told her to go and change her color. What I can't believe is that she *told* on him! Now you *know* she must have been mad at him for putting her through that trial. Can you imagine sitting there day after day, just listening, while all those women parade up there telling about how her husband was chasing after them? To say nothing of having everyone in D.C. seeing that video over and over of him and Rasheeda in the hotel room. Didn't she just bide her time, though! She sat there in court, day after day, with a stoic expression on her face, showing nothing. And then, she just bust wide open. And what is really interesting to me is that she knew exactly what to say to get the headline. Girl, how long do you think she had been angry at him for him telling her she didn't look right? Must have been a long time 'cause he has been mayor over ten years now. Man. She held in that anger all those years, and then, BOOM, she let him have it. With all this Rasheeda stuff, I just knew something had to come out. Don't you wonder what else she could tell?"

Even Du Bois —

On the very page where he denounced "inner racial distinction in the colored group" ("I resented the defensive mechanism of avoiding too dark companions in order to escape notice and discrimination in public"), W.E.B. Du Bois penned these words:

> I did not seek contact with my white fellow students [while at Harvard]. On the whole I rather avoided them. . . . Nor again was there any idea of racial amalgamation. I resented the assumption that we desired it. I frankly refused the possibility while in Germany and even in America gave up courtship with one "colored" girl because she looked quite white, and I should resent the inference on the street that I had married outside my race.

It is both amazing and profoundly disheartening to learn that even Du Bois did not understand that rejecting someone because of their color (dark) is the same as rejecting someone because of their color (light).

It is hard not to lose hope.

Men, Women, and Death

The fear, of course, is that I will get him killed.

We will be walking down the street together one day, happy, smiling, holding hands—a man with dark skin, a woman who is, they think, white. And one of the many crazy, violent white people in this country will take it upon himself to rectify a grievous social wrong.

A friend and I talked once about those first dates of our adolescence, about the excitement and the anxiety: "Do I look all right? What will I say? Will she/he like me?" But because my friend is a white black man, he also told me about the responses of those white adults who saw him walk into the school gym with his date, a teenage girl with brown skin. "There were hostile stares," he told me, "stares and angry mutterings." They saw them as an interracial couple, even though both teenagers were African American. And even though this African American boy had learned very

well the lesson "NEVER DATE WHITE," even though he had
learned it and was carefully following it, he was still wrong.
He was wrong if he "dated white," for he was black; and he
was wrong if he dated someone black, for he was "white."

I understood completely. It was a mess. But, I explained to
him, my situation was worse. Because if he was being perceived as a young white man dating an African American
girl, although he was not supposed to do that, he was still
"white," and therefore had the power, prestige, and social
standing of any other white man in this society. As a
"white" man, he had certain privileges, one of which was
being entitled to make decisions that others could not make.
Another was being entitled to the women of races, all of
whom had lower status than he. He was, after all, lord of the
American manor.

The same was not true of me and my date. For if there is
one survival lesson that an African American boy learns
early on, if there is one lesson that goes deep, it is that he
does *not* have access to white girls, white women. This is a
powerful taboo, and those who violate it put themselves in
terrible danger. A brown-skinned African American boy
who goes on a date with a white or "white" African American girl is engaging in risky business. You only need one
half-crazed, half-drunk keeper of the flame to mete out the
punishment. Does it really matter if the woman is "white" or
white? Would anyone stop to ask? Would they care? My
friend agreed: a date with me was much riskier business than
a date with him. (Small comfort to be right.)

It is hard to remember how these lessons are given, hard
to remember how we all learn these truths. The only verbal
lessons I recall receiving were as an adult, and surely there
were lessons before that. But I remember these two lessons
well, probably because they were so clear, so direct, so
accusatory.

The first lesson came at the wedding of white friends, a
wedding that I attended with the man I was then seeing, an
African American with dark skin. Weddings are such joyous

occasions that it hardly seemed to matter that we would not know most of the people there. We would meet the family and other friends of the bride and groom; we would all celebrate together. After the ceremony, my date and I went to the reception hall for dinner. And as we started to sit at our assigned table, a young white teenager already seated there stared at us, gasped, and said to me: "No! You're not supposed to be with him! White women are not supposed to be with black!" The rest of the guests at the table, family members, were embarrassed. We managed somehow to get through the meal. But I still remember the clarity of his understanding, for although he was a child with Down's syndrome, even he knew the rules. The only thing he didn't know was that he wasn't supposed to say it in public.

The second lesson I remember came from a black friend at a summer picnic in the park. Again, I attended with my date, a dark-skinned African American. We were all dressed for fun: I was wearing shorts, a tee shirt, sandals. And as we walked into the park to greet our friends — a cluster of black people at one picnic area surrounded by many groups of whites — this friend came up to us quickly and said, with an anxious tone, "Girl, you're going to get him killed dressed like that! Don't you have something you can put on to cover up?" He laughed nervously as he said it, trying to pretend that it was a joke. But we both knew full well that he meant it seriously. It was no joke.

I have thought a long time about his statement. It was very powerful and very frightening. I wondered if he was exaggerating the risk. Perhaps he was responding to his own sexual feelings as he looked at me, trying to dismiss them by dismissing me. Or did I really pose such a threat of danger at a picnic in a Washington, D.C., park on a summer's afternoon in the 1970s? That one African American man, at least, was clear: I could get someone — a black man — killed. And it would be all my fault for forgetting for an instant that I was "white" and that the rule for me was not to "date black."

It is more than bizarre to be black and to fear attack for being "white." Walking down the street in Berkeley, I was accosted by a homeless man who was irate when I did not respond to his entreaties: "You white bitch! You'll learn one day that black men are entitled to respect!" He followed me for a while, yelling and waving his fists in the air. A streak of pain ran through me — pain for him and for me.

This is my nightmare. It is during race riots in the city. I am in my car, trying to reach safety, and am pulled from the car and beaten by four young black men as I drive through a black neighborhood: "You white bitch!"

However, it is one thing to be stupidly killed by mistake. It is quite another to cause someone *else* to be stupidly killed by mistake — murdered because a white person thought a black man was violating the rules of racial purity by dating "white," by going out with me.

How does it happen that this is all my fault?

My anxiety soars.

Black Does Not
Equal Brown

It is a question we ask one another often—a familiar, easy question, a question asked so often we hardly notice we are asking it. We ask it when we leave the black community and move out singly, by twos, by threes, into the hostile whiteland—to a concert, a school meeting, a boat trip. Then, when we return home, home to our family, the black community, we are asked: "How many black people were there?"

I return from my first semester at college, and a friend of the family asks: "How many black students are there?" She is concerned: "Are you safe? Is your life hard? Do you have community?" I go to a conference of scholars in another city. A black professor at another school asks, "How many other black faculty are there with you?" He wonders, "Are you safe? How difficult is your life? Are they making you crazy?" We go to the park. Upon our return, a friend asks:

"Were there a lot of black people there?" She wonders if it would be safe for her to go there with her children. What are the chances of hostile looks, a fight, a ruined day?

I gauge the health of my mind and spirit by how I have answered that question in the past, and how I answer it now. In the past, when I was out in the world, I scanned the crowd unthinkingly, automatically counting the number of brown faces. I would interpret that to mean the approximate number of black people present. And there would always be the faint whisper of an idea that somehow I could not be counted in the same important way.

But now I answer that question differently. When someone asks me "How many black people were there?" I say, "I have no idea. How can you tell who is black? How can I?" For although I can count all the brown faces in a room, there is no way that I can count the "black" faces. For brown does not equal "black."

It is not that I don't know this and haven't always known this. But the full impact of this statement did not come to me until last year, when I heard a presentation by a civil rights lawyer. She was explaining the difficulty of developing statistical proof of discrimination based on sexual orientation when one does not know the number of gay people in the community at large. "How can you tell," she said, "when the fear of stigma and punishment means that many gay people will not tell you whether they are gay or not? There is simply no way to know how many people are gay. It could be that most people are."

I was stunned, amazed, thrilled. For she opened up my way of thinking about "black" Americans. Look around you now, today—in the grocery store, on the street, at the mall. Look carefully at the people on television. And think about what she said: "There is no way to tell." It could be that most of the people you are seeing are black.

You would think that I would always be able to tell who is black and who is not, as I am so carefully trained in the art of detecting race markers. Most black Americans are: we rely on these physical markers for self-preservation. We scrutinize the person's body, looking for a telltale cast to the skin, certain facial features, a specific hair texture. But there have been many times when even I did not know. I have been at social gatherings where I did not know a certain person was "black" until they dropped verbal markers into the conversation ("Are you a Delta too?"). I have had black colleagues I didn't know were black until someone else told me. And if this happens to me—if I can't tell who is black and who is white until someone lets me know—it also happens to you. It happens to us all. Indeed, sometimes (many times?), we are never told that a particular person is "black."

It is not, as some might argue, a question of "passing" for white, but a question of the need to know. Is there any particular reason for the firefighter to tell you he is black while he puts out the fire? Or for you to know that a particular ballerina dancing in the corps de ballet is black? Or for you to know that your child's periodontist is black? I know about these people because I know them and their families. I know that they consider themselves African American, that they are active in the black community. But if you do not know them on a personal basis, you would probably not know that they are black.

Not only do I know black people who are not brown, I also know black people who did not know they were black until they found out by accident in their later years. And I know of black people whose parents have decided to never tell them they are black. So tell me: how can you and I be sure when the players themselves do not know? Do not know *yet*? May never know? The most we can know for sure is that black does not equal brown. Brown is in our eyes; "black" is in our mind.

Here is a list of some people I know who are African Americans with white skin, black Americans generally mistaken for white:

    dentist
    firefighter

camp counselor
secretary
ballerina
college professor
corporate executive
police officer
lawyer
restaurant owner
basketball coach
high school teacher
factory worker
dress designer
filmmaker
historian
jewelry designer
teacher's aide
hotel manager
museum fund-raiser
corporate litigator
nurse
artist
writer
waitress
landlord
government worker
psychologist
elementary school teacher
psychiatrist
door-to-door salesman
forest service tour guide
babysitter
actress
doctor

And this is just *my* list—the list of one African American out of the 29,986,060 African Americans in this country. Suppose I asked the others to add to this list: how long would it be then? Or suppose we *looked* at the others: what color would they be?

Perhaps you have had professional dealings with one of these people. Perhaps you passed him on the street, saw her waiting in line to get into the theater. Perhaps you have seen the ballerina perform, been stopped by the police officer, asked questions of the nurse. Did you know they were black? Maybe the woman who waits on you at the restaurant this weekend will be black. How will you tell? Next time you watch television, try to guess which actors and actresses are black. Play a trick with your mind: assume for a moment that they are all African American. Does this vision make you anxious? unsettled? Or does this thrill you the way it thrills me?

My role in all this is not a popular one, for my task is to say over and over that, even on its own pathological terms, the racial purity system America has constructed does not work as planned. We African Americans have been here a long time now. We have been having children with Asian Americans and European Americans and Native peoples for more than four hundred years. And those physical traits that once marked one continent or another are no longer as clear as they once were. My role is to point out the paradoxes, to emphasize the contradictions until the system collapses of its own inanity.

But I am only one voice, and the dream of racial purity is still very valuable to those who own this country. It must be, will be, maintained. I roll the rock up the hill again and again, accepting the futility of my task. But I refuse to say that it makes sense. I refuse to say that brown equals "black." Ignoring this difference renders my position unclear and untenable, dismisses me. And I will not be dismissed.

Instructions

(For the "White" Person Who Wants to Understand)

A. How to Tell if a Person with White Skin Is "White"
   1. Ask the person.
   2. Assume that he or she will tell you the truth.
   3. Assume that he or she knows the truth.

B. How to Tell if You Are "White"
   1. Ask your parents.
   2. Assume that they know the truth.
   3. Assume that they will tell you the truth.

Lost Great-Uncle Charles

When we were children and did something particularly clever, my mother would say: "Why, you must be one of Mary Scales's granddaughters!" That was high praise indeed. "Mommie," my mother's mother, could do just about anything. She could sew whatever she put her mind to — upholstery, bedroom slippers, men's suits, pajamas. She cured an infected wound my "city doctor" had been treating for months, by tying a piece of fatback on it overnight. (I, a "city granddaughter," was mortified by these country ways. But it never hurt again!) She used to take me to the market with her to buy live chickens for supper. When we returned, she would swing them around her head until they were dead, then pluck their feathers over a huge steaming pot outside. She also cooked the best food in the world. I especially remember breakfast — fried fish, grits, brains and eggs, buttery griddle toast with homemade applesauce, fried bananas. And when there was a fretful baby in the house, she would just lay it up on her wide, wide bosom, pat its back, and rock for hours, satisfying them both.

I start this story with Mommie because I loved her, and because I like remembering my childhood summers in North Carolina. But I also start with her because that is where this story begins.

My grandmother, born Mary Mosby in 1881 in Burke-ville, Virginia, had three siblings: Ella, a half-sister; Clarence ("Unc" to us kids); and Charles, who ran away from home when he was a young man, to work on the railroad. Now in those days, the people who owned the railroads didn't hire "colored" workers, so the family understood this to mean that Charles had decided to pass over to the white side of his "family," the white part of the community—to pretend to be white. He was never heard of again.

I learned this fact only recently. And that is all I know of him: there are no pictures, no more stories. But recently a friend asked me, "Do you know anyone who is 'passing' for white? And did they ask you to keep their secret?" The an-swer is "no"—I have never met anyone who told me that they were pretending to be white. But I do have this one great-uncle I just learned about. So I decided to stop awhile and think about him—this relative I never met, this young man who left the family to go to work on the railroad and never came back.

The scholar G. Reginald Daniel considers passing for white one strategy of resistance for Americans of both Euro-pean and African descent. He calls it a way of "subverting the racial divide" by going underground. Although this is an interesting way to think of my great-uncle Charles, I don't see him this way, exactly. When I create a picture of him in my mind, I see him rather as an immigrant to a new country, "Whiteland," an immigrant who left the old country in search of a better life. Sometimes I think of him as an immi-grant who left home for economic gain. Because there were no jobs for him back in Sicily, in Dublin, in Haiti, in "Blackland," he left his friends and family, all he once held dear, and came over in steerage or in a handmade boat, or by hopping a freight train—quietly, secretly, late one night. Sometimes I see him as a political refugee who just got tired of being persecuted for holding the very dangerous political belief that he was, indeed, a man. And I can see him crossing his own Berlin Wall, with bullets spattering the dirt around him as he jumps down and runs away.

Most often, however, I think of him as an immigrant from Mexico, one man alone, slipping across the Rio Grande in the dark of night. He is like Diego who is leaving Mexico with the hope of a better life in Texas—Texas, now a part of the United States but land that once was part of Mexico, that once belonged to him. It is really quite curious. For Diego is traveling "back" to the land that once had been his but was stolen away, a land where he would now have to live in fear that someone would discover that he had returned to his own homeland. He was now an illegal alien. It was much the same for my great-uncle Charles. For just as South Texas belongs as much to this one immigrant from Mexico as it does to any Anglo in Texas, so too did "Whiteland" belong to my great-uncle Charles.

I wonder if it was hard for my great-uncle. Did he cry when he looked into his mother's eyes for the last time? When he said "goodnight" to his sisters and brother, knowing that they would not see each other ever again? Was he always and forever lonely for the places and people of his childhood? Or was he a trifling man, one who cared nothing about the people who cared for him?

I would probably be able to work up some anger toward this great-uncle if I thought that he had escaped to a good life in Whiteland and, in so doing, had left his family back in the old country, destitute and ill. If this were the case, and if he didn't even send money back home, I would consider him beneath contempt. This is simply not acceptable, whether one has emigrated from the Dominican Republic or Germany, Azerbaijan or Blackamerica. But in fact, that was not the case. Charles's sister Mary, my grandmother, married W. S. Scales, a man as enterprising as she. Although neither of them had more than a second-grade education, they were so successful in their various businesses that they managed to keep all four children in college during the Depression. His brother Clarence was manager of the Rex and the Lafayette, the two black theaters in Winston in those days. And his sister Ella was a teacher and administrator at the Fourteenth Street School.

So when I think of my great-uncle Charles, I don't think of him harming the family by leaving. Rather, I think of all *he* lost by leaving this wonderful family that raised me. I think about how mean a country must be to force someone to make such a cruel choice. And I wonder about his life after he left. I wonder if he settled down, earned a decent living, raised a family. I wonder if he ever told anyone he was "colored," if this secret weighed heavy on his heart — if once, just once, late one night, when his wife was fast asleep, if he leaned over and whispered his secret in her ear.

Or did he die young?

I like to think that he had a good life in this new land — that he learned the new language and the new ways, and that he survived. And because, like everyone else, I would rather my relatives be decent folk, not knaves, I also like to think that he did in fact "send something back" to his family in the old country. I like to think that he was the "white" man who stopped those white hoodlums from killing a black teenager whose car broke down in "their" neighborhood. He was the "white" merchant who hired black workers when no one else in town would. He was the anonymous donor who sent a hundred-dollar check to the black church after it was firebombed and those four little girls were killed. I like to think that he took care of all his family as best he could.

And I wonder — who are those "white" cousins whom I will never know?

On Being Like a Mule

> *It is impossible to look on a man and pretend that this man is a mule. It is impossible to couple with a Black woman and describe the child you have both created as a mulatto — either it's your child, or a child, or it isn't.*
>
> —*James Baldwin*

It wasn't until very recently, as I was looking up the spelling of the word "mulatto" in the dictionary, that I inadvertently discovered its derivation: "From the Spanish 'mulato,' young mule." Transfixed by those words on the page, I looked slowly down the column of words to find the definition of "mule":

"(myōōl), n.

1. The sterile offspring of a female horse and a male donkey, valued as a work animal, having strong muscles, a body shaped like a horse, and donkeylike large ears, small feet, and sure-footedness. . . .
2. Any hybrid between the donkey and the horse.
3. *Informal.* A very stubborn person.
4. *Bot.* any sterile hybrid. . . ."

"Sterile hybrid." What a ghastly term to apply to a person. It describes the result of a sexual union so unnatural, by species so unlike, that this creature is unable to meet one of the basic criteria of a species—the ability to reproduce. It describes a creature that will, happily, *not* be able to continue its unnatural line—a being that will die without offspring, so that the categories "horse" and "donkey" ("white," "black") will return to their former state of purity.

Sexual license across boundaries, with no social consequences—this is the dream of America.

I struggle to get a feeling for my namesake, the mule. My first thought is of Zora Neale Hurston's description of the black woman as "de mule uh de world"—the one who has to pick up the load and carry it for everyone else, white people and black men alike. I think of the mules in the Arizona copper mines who walked slowly down into the pitch-black mines, then slowly back up, laden with ore, year after year, never seeing the world outside of the mine, never seeing the light, until they went blind. A beast of burden. Slave-like. And stupid enough to accept slave treatment.

It is hard to think of anything positive about mules. They are not noble like horses, loyal like dogs, elegant like the lion. It was not mules who crossed the Alps to win a war for Hannibal. Mules are just there, stolid and stupid, strange-looking horses with ill-fitting ears.

Names are important. What people call us is important. Sometimes, when we name ourselves, the name says something about the person wearing the name. But, more often, we are named by others, and the name tells us something valuable about the namer.

In this case, the namer, America, calls me "mulatto," "like a mule." What does this tell us about America? What is gained by comparing those with ancestors from both Europe and Africa to a mule, a "sterile hybrid"? Actually, quite a lot. First of all, it makes clear that people from Africa and people from Europe are two different animal species, species that should lead separate lives, species that cannot be family. It also emphasizes the notion of hierarchy, for it seems obvious to me that our culture values horses more than donkeys. There are legends, poems, movies about horses; they are swifter, more lovely than donkeys. It is horses that are the superior creature in this unnatural couple. And what happens when this superior animal violates the normal order of things, transgresses strict boundaries to have sexual union with an inferior being, a creature of another species? Nature herself is offended, and condemns this union by presenting it with a deformed offspring — one that cannot reproduce. Thus, the image of the "sterile hybrid" — the mule, the mulatto — has enormous value. It teaches the lesson that America wants us all to remember. It reminds us of concepts of difference and opposition between African American and European American. It reinforces our understanding of the hierarchy of racial power and the importance of racial purity. And it tells us once again that sexual union between the two groups will not go unpunished.

In a country that considered it important to divide people by ancestry, in a country that decided to create a special name for those children born of the union of people from different lands, think of all the *other* words that could have been used! Imagine what new name could have been created if, instead of seeing this union as an attack on the dream of racial purity, America saw it as an opportunity to join two groups, much as royalty has used marriage to symbolize and consolidate the union of different groups of people. America could have then created a name to celebrate this union:

"people-who-link-us-together"
"people-who-join-our-families"
"people-who-bind-us-in-friendship"

Or, America could have seen these people as the forerunners of a new world, a world where all are linked through kinship:

"new people"
"people-of-the-future"

Or indeed, America could have looked at all the new, glorious skin colors created through the union of so many different kinds of people and celebrated this display of beauty:

"people-of-the-rainbow"

It would make me think of Joseph's coat of many colors. It would make me think of children returning home. It would make me think of God.

But no, we have only the mule, and the word "mulatto." We have only messages of opprobrium, disdain, ridicule — images of stupidity, slavery, and powerlessness. The young woman startled me with her rage. A European American with an African American child, she rejected the term outright. "I *hate* that word! It is so ugly. I will *not* use it for my child." She's right, of course. She doesn't have to use that word. Ever. None of us do.

I recently attended a conference at which African American scholars from many disciplines came together to discuss issues of ethnicity, color, and gender as they pertain to African American identity. How exciting to be part of a group that finally wanted to address these hard, hard questions within our community! Because the discussion concerned color, there was some debate during the sessions about the use of the word "mulatto." Some refused to use it, noting its insulting connotations. Others used it, but pointed out that they did so only because it was an important historical word that had been used extensively in the literature of race and color: they could not address that literature without using that term. This all seemed thoughtful and well-reasoned to me.

But it was there, for the first time, that someone named me "a hankety-haired yellow heifer." Well, no — not me directly, but it *felt* direct, because the dark-skinned scholar who made the reference in her presentation was angry when she made it. She was angry because a white black woman — a nineteenth-century writer — had made derogatory comments in her writing about black Americans with dark skin. Now this scholar laughed when she said the words, as if to diminish their force. She also apologized before using it, and called it "a phrase from my youth," as if it was really not her using those words that day. But it was. It was a phrase she used to wound, and she meant it for that moment and for the pain she felt that day.

I have decided not to travel down the path of trying to figure out all that she meant by naming me after yet another farm animal: a heifer, a "hankety-haired yellow heifer." I know enough. It sure wasn't good.

(Dis)Continuities

I read a story once about a place in Florida where you can
swim with dolphins. They keep them in a penned-in lagoon
on a bay. For about twenty-five dollars, you can spend an
hour frolicking in the water with your fellow mammals. I
was enchanted with the idea, for I love the water and I love
swimming. I'm sure I romanticize the idea of dolphins as
kindly, playful water creatures, but I still love the idea. Some
years ago, on my third trip under the ocean in scuba gear, I
stroked and hand-fed a large fish. It helped me make the
connection between animals on the land and animals in the
ocean. So I read more about this dolphin playground — perhaps I would go one day. And then I saw the most amazing
thing. The owner of the site reported that when human
swimmers join the dolphins they usually all cavort in the water together. But when a pregnant swimmer joins them, the
female dolphins shove the male dolphins out of the way and

swim with her, one female dolphin on one side, one on the other, until she leaves the water. One visitor was astonished. "How can they tell I'm pregnant?" she exclaimed. "I just found out myself last week!" The trainer explained that the dolphins can hear the second heartbeat. They recognized her as kind, another pregnant swimming mammal, and took her in. But another time, a swimmer who was pregnant with twins joined the dolphin lagoon. The dolphins heard three heartbeats instead of two, and they acted differently. They did not swim by her side to provide support and protection. They shunned her. A strange-looking water mammal with one heartbeat, even two, was enough the same to be kind. A strange-looking water mammal with three heartbeats was not.

A friend once explained to me much the same phenomenon with respect to people with physical disabilities. She described the hierarchy of power and acceptability within that community as one based on the degree to which one looks and acts like an able-bodied person. As she explained it, the person who is the least acceptable is the one who looks the least the same, or the one who does not move in the same, "normal" way, but in a jerky way. "Who is this person? What is he likely to do? I do not recognize him. I fear him." On the other hand, a person in a wheelchair is most "the same." One could imagine, for example, that he is sitting in a chair at a desk, at a dinner party, in the living room. He looks "normal." The degree of difference is slight. And I use the pronoun "he" advisedly, for according to my teacher the approximation of "normal" includes not only physical (dis)ability, but also sex and race. Because white men in wheelchairs are most like those found acceptable by the larger community, they are also the most acceptable within the disabled community.

Television confirms her analysis—television, which shows us what perfect people look like when they are not quite perfect, when they are almost the same, not too different. Television shows us pictures of the disabled now and then. We see them generally in offices, and we see that they are indeed white men in wheelchairs. They are just disabled enough for the television producers to get points for putting them on, and not so disabled that they are too different, not so different that they move way out in the margin.

I try to understand questions of color within this context of the degree of difference. At what point does sameness become difference? At what point does continuity become discontinuity? How far into the margin is too far?

Television teaches us that the degree of difference must be small, but that it must show. If the viewer can't see the wheelchair, it doesn't count. So if you are going to portray a black person, or an Asian, the person must have dark skin, or must have eyes with epithelial folds. A black person with blond hair or blue eyes wouldn't do, any more than an Asian American with blond hair and blue eyes. There is a correct and acceptable degree of difference. You may fit within one category or another, but don't get too different. And don't get too same. Don't blur the margins.

But we do blur the margins. We are more different than is acceptable. We exist in ways that confuse the categories. And categories are acceptable; a continuum is not. I try to imagine what it must be like to meet someone who is white and black, a black white person. Like Michelle Cliff's "Girl from Martinique," who painted herself a checkerboard black and white and sits on a throne in the circus sideshow, we are the freaks, the water mammal with three heartbeats. I imagine that there is a sense in which my whiteness is less disquieting to white people because of the degree of sameness, and less disquieting to blacks because white people are known. And yet at the same time, it must be more disquieting, because my sameness is not a true sameness, and my whiteness expresses things both known and unknown.

While I sit at a remove, watching how badly people around me deal with differences of race and color, I must tell you that I am more than conscious of my own limitations with respect to difference. I am most aware of it when it comes to physical difference, for I was raised with differences of race and color, and it is the unknown that frightens. It is people whose bodies do not fit neatly into the category of bodies as I know them who make me the most anxious. I turn the page in *Ebony*. Suddenly, unexpectedly, I am looking into the eyes of two sisters joined at the head, smiling into the camera. "They have just started college. They have lots of friends. Isn't life grand!" I am enraged at the magazine editors. I turn the page quickly, refusing to look at them, refusing to participate in their exploitation. Or do I simply refuse to acknowledge their existence? This is not how things are supposed to be. This is not how bodies are supposed to look.

Some pictures won't leave my mind. They are printed there for all time. I am sorry they are there, and you might be angry at me for showing you this picture. It was just this month, at the airport, as I was walking through the corridor to a connecting flight, that I saw a man. At first, I could not understand what I saw. Why were his legs angled out like chicken legs from his hips? Why did his feet look like chicken feet? Where were his shoes and socks? And then I realized that, no, those were not his legs, those were not his feet — those were his arms, his hands, fingers splayed out to walk on. For this man had no feet, no legs, no body below his waist. A young man, neatly dressed, with brown hair and a lovely, sad face.

I did not break stride.

But I am haunted by my picture of him. I was aghast, stunned, repulsed by how different he was from me. He did not fit comfortably into my category "man," which I thought I had seen as a broad, widely encompassing word. He did not really fit into my category "person," even "disabled person." He was in his own category, somewhere in the margin — way out in the margin. And I was repulsed by my new understanding of myself.

I'm sure that if I got to know him I could expand my category "person" to include him. I would be able to incorporate him into my world of community, family, people like me. But I don't know him. I had not seen someone who looked like him before. He was the water creature with three heartbeats. And I see once again how difference at the margin frightens us. As the anthropologist Mary Douglas explains: ". . . all margins are dangerous. If they are pulled this way or that the shape of fundamental experience is altered."

Douglas tells us that when a deformed child is born to a Nuer woman, the Nuer see it as a monstrous birth: the child has transgressed the boundaries between people and animals. In order to resolve this tension, they relabel the child — it was really a baby hippopotamus, born into the wrong family. And they return the child to the water, his true home, where he belongs. Thus the boundaries of the categories are kept pure, and order is restored.

That is not our way. We do not kill those who do not fit within the categories we create. We marginalize, we reject, we shun. We hide them away. There might well be many more young men like the man in the airport hidden in homes, in veterans' hospitals around the country, afraid of how they will be treated if they come out. For the categories must remain pure. Life must be understandable. "The quest for purity," Douglas writes, "is pursued by rejection." She is right. It is we who put that sadness into his eyes. It is you who put it in mine.

I return to the water for comfort and peace. I recall another day, many years ago, at the ocean. In the ocean. It was the first time I had ever used goggles and a snorkel. It was the first time I had even come close to seeing into the world of the sea. I was swimming in a clear bay in the Caribbean, warmed by the sun, embraced by the water.

At some distance from shore were giant rocks, some thirty, forty feet high. I don't remember all that I saw as I looked down into the water through my goggles — probably small rocks and shells embedded in the sand, seaweed, perhaps fish darting around. I do remember my delight at feeling that even though I was only on the edge of the sea I was beginning to understand its nature. What I remember most about this first trip, however, was those massive gray rocks in the distance that at first seemed so forbidding. And this will sound trivial. You will say, "How can she have not understood this before?" But that afternoon, I finally saw and understood the wholeness of the rocks, for I could see not only the tops of them, above the water, but also the rest of them, underneath the water, on the ground. I could see that they were not mysterious objects, somehow perched out there, on the sea. I finally understood that the land under the water where those rocks stood was the same land I had been walking on earlier. Because I had looked at those huge rocks from another angle, I could see the connections. I saw the continuities, instead of the discontinuities. The line of demarcation I had formerly seen vanished. There were no separate systems, sea and land, either clear or blurred at the margins. There was only one category, one system, and it was whole.

The Re-Vision of Marginality

When the subject comes up, I tell people that it was "in a former life" that I was a student and teacher of French. It seems like that long ago.

And it was even longer ago than that when I started my love affair with the French language. I was probably about seven or eight, the adoring follower of my older sister, Kay, and her best friend, Jane. Jane was studying French in school. Sometimes, when the two big girls were off by themselves, I would look through Jane's schoolbooks, wistfully. I must have thought that if I could learn French, I could be like her — worldly, sophisticated, an artist — and all of fourteen!

I was lucky. Although I was always hopelessly confused by mathematics and science, I had a gift for languages. I still remember how much I enjoyed Latin I, my first language course, in junior high school. I loved it all — the declensions

(Mr. Brockway waved his arms and led our chant: "hic, haec, hoc; huius — three — times . . ."), the orderliness, the thrill of decoding a sentence. When I started French in high school, I discovered I had a "good ear." I could hear and reproduce the tonal and rhythmic subtleties of a foreign language.

By then, I was hopelessly in love with all things French — music and movies, books, magazines, newspapers. As a high school student, when I went to the French bookstore in Rockefeller Center, it was as if I had arrived in the Holy Land. I mooned around the bookshelves, fingering the uncut pages of books published by Gallimard and Hachette, eavesdropping on the conversations of real French people just steps away. In my freshman year of college I took my first literature course ever — a course in French literature. In this class, I was swept away by a deepened appreciation of literature, as well as by Emma Bovary's passion for Rodolphe. I adored the tragic poetry of Baudelaire and Gérard de Nerval ("Je suis le ténébreux, le veuf, l'inconsolé . . ."). I spent one college summer studying and living with a French family in Aix-en-Provence. And because it was the 1960s, and because I was at Oberlin College, my passion for all things French was transmuted into a passion for the liberation of Algeria, which we read about in magazines from French Africa as well as in the leftist French paper *Express*.

My love affair was well rewarded. There was a certain cachet to being able to speak French, to being bilingual and bicultural, to having lived, even for a short time, in France. It was assumed that I had a certain knowledge about French culture and style, that I knew certain things about French politics and daily life.

This obsession with French language and culture was my own choice, a very personal passion. But there is no doubt that it was created and encouraged by a society that values and rewards learning other languages and learning about other cultures. My interest was also valued and rewarded by my friends and family. Relatives could introduce me to their friends, with some admiration: "Now, this is Judy. She speaks French!" It was considered quite acceptable that I knew everything about French literature and nothing about American or English literature. It was considered charming when I sometimes thought of a word in French before I could remember it in English. It was a social coup that I could not only cook "blanquette de veau à l'ancienne," but also understood the French on a restaurant menu and said it correctly for the French waiter, who would beam at my pronunciation. The lesson society taught me, then, was that being bilingual and bicultural was not only exciting but also valuable. I was well on my way to being bilingual, and this fact was applauded all around.

We are lucky in this country. We don't have to cross the Atlantic or travel thousands of miles to study another rich culture. We have many right here. But the same lessons are not taught with respect to African American culture — a culture with a rich history, with important intellectual and artistic traditions. One might expect that, given the value America places on learning about other cultures, in every high school, along with the traditional four-year sequence on Euro-American culture, there would be a four-year sequence on the language, history, and literature of African Americans. One would expect that the teacher would do just what I did when I taught French to high school students. Along with presenting the substantive material, the teacher would arrange field trips, set up musical presentations, invite guest speakers, set aside special days for cooking and eating the food from this culture, create ever-changing wall displays, have students subscribe to newspapers and magazines, and organize plays and musical events for families and community. And as with French, white parents would push school principals to include these lessons as early as first grade. As with French, the high school curriculum on African America would be tested in statewide exams. As with French, white parents would be delighted if their children "slipped" for a moment, and thought that they were black; and black parents would be delighted if their children did the same. And all the children would grow up being praised and admired for being bilingual and bicultural, black and white, in America.

I suppose you're laughing by now! And why not? That is surely not the way it works. The culture of African Americans is not considered as valuable as the culture of the French. The reason is clear. Unlike the French and the Americans, these two groups, black and white, are at war. And the valuation of culture is one of the most important tools of combat. A white student who becomes bilingual and bicultural black/white is probably punished by his parents, not praised. (Can you imagine the stir it would create in her family if a white college student told her parents that she wanted to major in African American literature?) And a black student who becomes bilingual and bicultural, black/white, is often considered suspect by members of the black community who become anxious if white America is engaged too deeply. (This is a true story: The black students at a predominantly white college formally voted Heather "out of the race" after she joined the school's debating team.)

We must do better than this. And an important way to start is to take control of the business of definition and valuation.

For years, I accepted the definition of others. I believed that, as a white black American, both inside and out of both black and white communities, my life was a prime example of what sociologists call "marginal" — someone who is on the margin of two major groups but a member of neither. This is clearly not a joyous place to be. But I have decided not to reinforce this view of me by accepting it. I prefer a more positive definition. And I think that if you turn the word "marginal" over, you find the word "bilingual" — and at the same time you emphasize inclusion and richness rather than exclusion and isolation. So I have decided to hark back to the great American lesson that it is valuable, and a great advantage, to be bilingual and bicultural. It is better to see and hear the world in stereophonic wide wrap-around sound, than in mono. If one has been placed in the middle of everything that is going on, why not enjoy it? And I do. I am as moved by Schubert's Trout Quartet as I am by the songs of Sweet Honey in the Rock. I weep when I hear a choir sing "Precious Lord, Take My Hand," and I am filled with joy when I hear Puccini's "Messa di Gloria." I embrace all the treasures these two cultures offer me. Why choose less, when one could have more? And why cheat our children out of all this richness?

The truth is that it is easy to be bicultural and bilingual. And the truth is that this is easy to teach, and we teach it in school all the time. There is really no great need for new course material or workshops or planning sessions on diversity. This is old stuff. Schools have been teaching students to value other cultures and learn other languages for hundreds, probably thousands, of years. The only real question is whether America wants to teach its youth to value African American culture, Latin American culture, Native culture, Asian American culture. Does America want all its children so bilingual and bicultural that they have access to the deep richness of these cultures? Do we want our children to be so steeped in these cultures that a black child might slip and ask her mother to pass the "papas" instead of the "potatoes"? That an Asian American girl might get frustrated because she can't figure out how to corn-row her hair? That a little white boy might say to his mother, who has just picked him up from a party at a black classmate's house, "Mom, did you feel funny being the only white person there?"

We don't have to glorify the borders and the margins. We can all be bilingual and bicultural in many different ways. And it is a rich, rich way to be in the world.

Affirmative Action and Stigma: The Education of a Professor

At the age of forty-four, I changed careers and communities when I left the civil rights community in Washington, D.C., for the academic world in western New York. The move was hard. It was not only the career change, the geographic dislocation, the social disruption that were difficult. It was also the move from a black city — and a community of civil rights lawyers within that city — to the white world of academia. Instead of working in tandem with black and white attorneys on a civil rights agenda, I was teaching civil rights law in a white workplace that had its own unknown agenda. I was teaching in a workplace with twelve black faculty on tenure track out of a total of 1,200 faculty members. I would be the second black woman out of that group.

Here in the academic world I have been forced to think hard thoughts about my entitlement to be a part of this community. I have also had to think about the entitlement of latino and black students to belong. Here in the academic world I have learned hard lessons about affirmative action and stigma.

The reason my education as a professor has been so profound has to do, I think, with numbers. The white community in Washington, D.C., although powerful, is a numerical minority in a black city. It is therefore not very forthright when speaking about its privilege. It has learned to curb its tongue, to speak in nonracist ways to black listeners. In academia, the white community has not learned that lesson. As an overwhelming numerical majority, it has not had to. It has thus taught me better — better than I had expected, better than I had wanted. It is those lessons that I write about now, in an effort to understand them and to diminish their control over my life.

Let me start out by stating that I agree with Jesse Jackson: There is nothing new about affirmative action. In this country there has been affirmative action for white men for more than three hundred years. All we are trying to do now is balance things out by changing the beneficiaries of affirmative action for a while. Thus, when we talk about affirmative action, we are not talking about special treatment for people of color or for white women. We are talking about equal treatment — three hundred years for them, three hundred years for us. White men got good jobs and good pay for three hundred years because of their race and sex. Now it is our turn to get access to those same benefits, also because of our race and sex.

But somehow, in the transposition, things get murky and muddy. Somehow the clear, clean concept of "turnabout is fair play" gets lost. All of a sudden, there is talk of who is qualified and who is not. All of a sudden, there is stigma.

Although this is something I recognized for years, I relearned it in an overt and dramatic way from my students. I remember in particular one session in a course on employment discrimination law, when I was introducing the concept of affirmative action. The case we were discussing was the *Weber* case, where Kaiser Aluminum and the steel-workers' union had jointly created a craft training program to remedy the historic exclusion of blacks from craft positions. They would admit black and white workers, one for one, until the training program was full. I had planned to use that class time to discuss how the Supreme Court had reached the conclusion that creating such a program did not violate Title VII of the 1964 Civil Rights Act, which prohibits basing employment decisions on the race of the worker. Oddly enough, we never got to that discussion. The entire hour was spent on the concerns of white students about the lack of qualifications of the black workers. And what is really remarkable about their concerns is that in *Weber* no one was qualified and no one was expected to be qualified to do the job: that is precisely the point of a training program.

Now it is true that Brian Weber, the white worker who filed suit because he was not allowed into the program, did have more seniority than some of the black workers who were selected, but this only speaks to the fact that Kaiser had undoubtedly discriminated with respect to hiring — of course black workers would have less seniority overall than white workers. Even then, relative seniority does not speak to the basic question of qualifications — that is, to the question of who can do the job. And it certainly does not speak to the question of who can be trained for the job. But somehow the white students in the class could not let go of that issue. "Affirmative action" meant "unqualified." The notion of qualifications had such a hold on them that the facts of the case became irrelevant.

I remember, in another course, discussing the affirmative action hiring and promotion order entered by the federal district court in Buffalo, New York, with respect to long-standing discrimination by the Buffalo police and fire departments. Because the hiring and promotion exams were shown to have an adverse impact on the hire and promotion of black, hispanic, and white female candidates, and because the city was unable to show that the exams were related to the jobs in question, the court ordered a one-for-one hiring quota of black and white candidates who had passed the exam, but without regard to their scores on those exams. Again, the white students were outraged. "Unqualified!" they cried. But how could the question of qualifications even be addressed, I argued, if the city could not show any connection between the exam and doing the job? Again, the fact that there was no validation of the exam was irrelevant to them.

Let me tell you one more story about affirmative action and qualifications and stigma. It is a true story, about a conversation that took place on my arrival in academia. As I began to learn about the nature of the tenure struggle, a colleague (a white male colleague) was denied tenure. He came into my office soon afterward to offer advice about tenure, to share lessons learned from his loss. "The pace of publishing is important," he said. "I waited too long to publish my first piece, and they lost confidence in me as a scholar. Be sure to publish early." "What a gift," I thought. "How kind of him to reach out through his pain to help a novice." He gave more suggestions, then concluded: "But really, you don't need to worry, because you're black. You will get tenure anyhow." His statement hit me like a smack across the face. How dare he try to invalidate all my past and future work so easily! I stammered a response: "If that is so, why have none of the black law professors who came here before me been granted tenure?" But once again, the facts seemed irrelevant, a feeble answer to his charge — a charge that my work would not be judged on merit, a charge that the only reason he did not get tenure was because he was white (because, surely, his credentials were impeccable), a charge that the only reason that I might get tenure was because I was black. Irrefutable charges, both. Perhaps he was right. And how would I ever know? Or was it ultimately impossible to know?

This is the connection between affirmative action and stigma: "You were only allowed in this job because you are

black. You will only get tenure because you are black. You
would never get anything otherwise, because you are not
otherwise qualified." And this is a good example, because it
shows the dynamics of that interaction. It shows that it is a
tool used by those who feel threatened and weak to attack
those who are vulnerable. It shows that it is a convenient,
ever-present tool that can be used against a convenient, ever-
present victim. It is new language, but it is an old dynamic,
an old victim, and an old story. The story used to go like
this:

> "You *can't* get the job *because* you are not qualified.
> Everybody knows that black people are stupid."

Now the story has a new beat. Now it sounds like this:

> "You *can* get the job *even though* you are not quali-
> fied. Everybody knows that black people are
> stupid."

Stigma does not grow out of affirmative action. Affirmative
action redefined as special help for the unqualified is merely
a new way of reinforcing stigma. A tool to remedy social
injustice becomes a tool to reinforce that same injustice. And
we are reminded that those who create the stigma turn every
event, every action, to that end, even the proposed remedy.

In this dynamic, then, it becomes clear that there are two
possibilities if one wants a particular job (or tenure, or ad-
mission to college, or a promotion). Either one gets the job
because one is also a member of a stigmatized group, or one
does not get the job, again because one is a member of a
stigmatized group. Stigma is constant. The only question,
then, is this: "Do you want the job or not?" Some say "no,"
and opt out. Like Richard Rodriguez, who was appalled that
he received so many teaching offers

> ("After all, not many schools are going to pass up the
> chance to get a Chicano with a Ph.D. in Renaissance
> literature.")

while his fellow graduate students received none, some decide the game is not worth the candle and try to live outside the labeling:

> "My decision was final. No, I would say to them all. Finally, simply, no."

But what then of the rest of us? What if you decide that you *do* want the job? It is one thing to be willing to use the people who are using you—they want to hire people of color, or white women, for whatever reason. Does it then follow that you were hired only because of your status and not because of your qualifications? And once you have started down that line of "reasoning," the problem becomes one of self-validation. And then the problem becomes one of getting your work done. When the stigma so affects one's sense of self—the very source of ideas and creativity and energy—it is easy to see the problem of getting one's work done. In fact, it is a wonder that any work gets done at all. Perhaps this is what Countee Cullen was alluding to when he wondered what God could have been thinking of

> "To make a poet black, and bid him sing!"

How can one live inside the stigma, and yet remain enough untouched by it to do one's work? How can we live inside the stigma and still "sing"? How can we fight against the stigma, fight against the belief that we are "unqualified," and still retain enough energy and belief in ourselves to enable us to get our work done? This is hard, but clearly it can be done. Black poets *do* sing.

One way to survive at living and working within stigma is to keep in close contact with others who wear that stigma, to try to see each other honestly, and to give each other the encouragement and honest assessment of our work that we all need. Many minority and white women law professors do this for each other. I have also found it helpful to read about the lives of those who have retained a strong sense of self and found the energy to "sing." How could one read about the Grimké sisters, Anna Julia Cooper, Malcolm X, or Mary Church Terrell without being inspired to keep on with our work. And literature also helps. The words of writers like James Baldwin, Lucille Clifton, and Sandra Cisneros can bring wonder, understanding, and nourishment into our lives.

There is a danger, however, in being successful at this. The oppressor groups expend enormous energy creating and maintaining the purity of these categories and definitions. If society has stigmatized you and you act as if you are not stigmatized, you are violating some serious social norms. Stigma is used for a reason — for social structure and for social control. It tells you what your place is, and it tells you to stay in your place. And there is dislocation, there is confusion, there is rage if you act in inappropriate ways. There is a sense in which you are "out of control" (out of *its* control, that is). And society does not tolerate well those who are out of control.

I have seen this dynamic manifest itself in academia through white colleagues' insistence on stigma, both for minority students and faculty. I offer two examples. The first incident took place during my first year in academia, when, like most newcomers, I often floundered and erred. A university administrator told me that when she asked a white colleague if he would help me, he explained he could not because he didn't know how to talk to me: I was "not from the street." My sameness was thus raised as a barrier: Only if I were more clearly different, operating within the stigma (that is, "under control"), would I receive support.

Students are harmed the same way. I once saw white colleagues consider denying a benefit to a latino student precisely because of his impressive background (graduate degree, professional experience, board memberships), when white students with similar backgrounds were found acceptable. When I protested, one admitted that I was right: white faculty members did prefer minority students who seemed "different" (weaker, lesser), even though that was not fair.

And he reminded me that I should not forget to start from the presumption that all white people are racists. I have not forgotten his lesson. You will be punished for failing to operate by the rules of control, for failing to act within the stigma.

You will also be punished by the members of the stigmatized group who have become used to the stigma and accept it as a part of their own identity. For shifting the definition of self is too hard, and seeing others make the shift becomes too painful a reflection of who one has become. I remember arguing with other black members of the law school admissions committee, in favor of admitting a black applicant with a B average from a top-ranked college who had taken a lot of courses in the history and literature of black Americans. "Her B average doesn't mean much," they insisted. "Look at the meaningless, easy courses she has taken." "Since when are history and literature courses 'easy' courses?" I asked. The answer was that "everyone knew" there is nothing to these courses. Well, in a sense they were right. Everyone in a racist society is supposed to know that anything the oppressed group has accomplished is of little merit. And many in the oppressed group have so internalized that "knowledge" that they will take it on themselves to punish those who refuse to "know" that truth.

So here is the dilemma: You are punished if you are controlled by the stigma, for then you cannot get your work done. And you are punished if you transcend the stigma, for then you *can* get your work done. Society has created a "lose–lose" situation for us. What we have to do is turn that situation around and see it for the free-ing gift that it is. The best way I can think of to describe that freedom is to describe Merle, a friend and former colleague. A white woman raised in a professional family in the south, Merle lived what I viewed as a very free life. While practicing law full-time in Washington, D.C., she also lived by herself on a farm in Virginia, a two-hour drive away, where she raised chickens and vegetables, repaired old farm buildings, and kept her Dobermans in line, with toughness and grit. Once, when I asked her how she got so free to choose her own life, she explained that in the world of white Southerners the boundaries are very narrow and very precise. Once you step over those boundaries, you are *completely* outside. You might as well be a mile away from the line, as a foot. It makes no difference — out is out. And once she became a civil rights lawyer, she was definitely on the other side of the line. There was no way she would ever get back inside. It didn't even matter if she stood close to that line. She was thus "free" to go as far as she wanted.

So I think about Merle, who found a path to personal freedom by being stigmatized and locked out. And I think that maybe there is something helpful in that for us. We can let the stigma eat us alive. Or we can look at it, walk away from it, and sing.

Skinwalkers, Race, and Geography

In Navajo cosmology there exist certain powerful creatures who, although they appear to be mere humans, can change shape whenever they wish by taking on animal form. These are supernatural beings, not like you and me. They are called "skinwalkers."

And I think about them, and this name, when I think about how we all "skinwalk" — change shapes, identities, from time to time, during the course of a day, during the course of our lives. I think about how we create these identities, how they are created for us, how they change, and how we reconcile these changes as we go along.

A young woman leaves her family on the farm and goes to medical school, where she learns a new language, a new culture. She tells me that she feels like an immigrant in a new land. She feels as if she is changing skin, shifting shape, and will be forever shifting as she travels back and forth between these two worlds. A young man goes to visit his parents with a wife and new child. He visits, however, in a complicated way, as he is now not only a son but also a husband and a father. And he shifts identities during the visit, mediating between these different roles within his newly structured family. A child whose parents have different religious beliefs — the father Methodist, the mother Episcopalian; the mother Roman Catholic, the father Greek Orthodox; the father Reform Jew, the mother Buddhist — this child learns to change shape as she communicates in two languages with her parents, as she visits with different sets of grandparents, aunts and uncles, cousins, during the holidays. And I, when I moved from a predominantly black civil rights community in Washington, D.C., to a predominantly white university in Buffalo, I too was a "skinwalker." In Washington, in the black community within a black city, I was a woman who just happened to be black. But in the Buffalo academic world, in this white community within a white city, I became a black person who just happened to be a woman.

All of these examples involve moving from one place to another, from one life to another, from one culture, one role, to another. But sometimes you can change identities while you are doing absolutely nothing at all. Things change around us. Society changes its rules and its boundaries, and suddenly you take on a different form: you become a heron, or forsythia, or your ancestor.

I have been thinking for a long time about two young girls, girls who were skinwalkers, sisters who never met.

The first, Marie, lived in Thionville, a small village in eastern France, in 1871. Like all good French girls, she went to Mass with her family, went to confession, and wore a beautiful white dress to her first Communion. Because her family had a prosperous farm, she also went to a small school, where she studied the French kings and queens, read the plays of Corneille and Racine, and learned the old songs of the region. Then one bright fall day, one day while she was in the kitchen with her mother putting bread on the table for the midday meal, somewhere far away, in some office or lawmaking place, one of the people who get to draw the lines wrote something down on a piece of paper — and suddenly Marie had a different identity. She was no longer French. She was German.

How could she comprehend this? Was she really supposed to unlearn everything she had ever learned about who she was? About who her people were? That must be so, because Germany immediately installed German schools in its new territory, the former French province of Lorraine. And suddenly Marie, now German, was required to speak only German and study the glory of German history.

The second young girl, Hannah, lived on her family farm in the Tidewater area of Virginia in 1785. Both her parents were free Negroes. Her father worked as a carpenter, and the whole family worked their small farm, a farm that provided a good life for Hannah and her two sisters. With the other black children in the community, the girls learned reading and writing and Bible verses in classes held in the nearby black church — the center of religion, culture, and community for all Negroes, free and enslaved, who lived in the Tidewater area in those days. And after classes, the children played circle games together, and they sang the old work songs and spirituals their grandparents had taught them. Then one day, one muggy summer's day while Hannah was sitting at the kitchen table with her mother stringing beans for dinner, something happened miles away, something that would change her life forever. The Virginia legislature changed the line between black and white. Now before this time, Hannah and her sisters were black, because one of their great-grandparents was black. They thus met the statutory definition of "Negro" in 1784. But in 1785 the legislators redefined "Negro" to mean anyone who had one black grandparent. And this, Hannah didn't have. All her grandparents were white. So on that simple summer's day, while she was at her home on the farm, someone somewhere wrote three sentences on a piece of paper and, magically, supernaturally, Hannah, a "skinwalker," became "white."

Thinking about the lives of these two young girls—one whose life was thrown into disarray by lines drawn on a map; the other, who was turned inside out by lines marked down in a book of rules—thinking about these two girls makes me think about the relationship between race and geography.

In both instances, we are talking about an exercise in drawing lines, lines to separate Here from There. The line-makers are marking boundaries, borders, creating Insiders and Outsiders. They are creating an "us" and a "them." They are creating the Other. Also, in both instances, those who draw these lines are drawing pictures of the world. They are showing what the world looks like, how the world *should* look, what looks right to them. So if you study their picture, you will know who you are—black or white, French or German, "us" or "them."

All this means, of course, that the line-drawers have the authority to describe the world for everyone in it. They are exercising enormous power, power they have grabbed or earned or received or simply found. But they have it, this power to locate the line, to decide who stands where in relationship to the line, and to divide community resources based on that decision.

Thus, whether we are talking about race or geography, marking boundaries creates property rights, for it is the boundaries that define who gets what—who gets the most, who gets less, who gets nothing—who takes, and who gets taken. And whether we are talking about race or geography, both imply war, as property rights always do. For those who somehow have the power to draw these lines, the power to say that they will get the most, will then have to, in fact *must*, fight to maintain those lines. And that means war.

Race and geography have one more important trait in common. They are both equally arbitrary systems of (dis)organization. Whether a person is sitting at a desk drawing lines on a piece of paper that represents the surface of this planet, or putting marks on a piece of paper that form words telling how to separate humans one from the other — no matter which task one is engaged in, it is simply and only a task. It is not a given, not a fact, not an eternal truth. Also, it is a task that leads to other tasks. For after creating this idea and drawing this line, the line-drawers must then convince a lot of people that this is the right line to draw and an important line to draw. And then they must develop a system to maintain these lines.

This is a lot of work.

Just think of the time, energy, and resources that a country uses to create and maintain the lines between its tribe and the tribe on the other side of the line. First, there are probably wars to establish the lines. Then you have to have guards on patrol at all times to make sure that only certain people cross the line. And there are immigration rules and lawyers and border patrols and enforcement agencies and soldiers and sailors and pilots and planes and bombs. The country also spends enormous sums of money teaching its youth about the importance, the "rightness" of the tribal line, so they will be eager to guard the line when it is their turn to patrol.

Then realize that this is the same amount of time and energy we expend to maintain the lines of racial purity in this country. And it is done the same way. There have been fights on the battlefield. And there are still fights — in the courts, in legislatures, on the streets of America — a continuing struggle to maintain the line between black and white, to reinforce its validity and power. The country has published rules, drafted forms, hired census-takers, created grandfather clauses and gerrymandering and segregated water fountains and back-of-the-bus and "cordons sanitaires." It has deputized all Americans who are not black to engage in this battle as soon as the boat brings them here from Peru, from Ireland, from Japan. Similarly, white America expends enormous resources in school and in the media to teach its youth about the intrinsic rightness of this line, so that they will not question its value when they reach the age to stand guard.

One task is overt; the other, covert. But line-drawing is line-drawing. It is the same task.

So the next time you say "black" or "white," the next time you hear someone use a racial designation, think about geography. And when you think about geography, see this picture:

> There is a small group of men in a tent, and it is night. These men, lieutenants and cartographers, are sitting, standing around a small table, trying to calculate where to put the line. An oil lamp on the table reflects its yellowish light on their tired faces, on papers strewn about. The men are concentrating on one of these papers—a heavy parchment scroll, its red wax seal broken. The scroll is from the generals at the front, claiming victory, and it tells the mapmakers what to do. The scroll says this:
>
> Draw the line here.
> We have taken more land.
> This much is ours.

"Where're Your People From?": Thoughts on Ethnicity and Race

As a single woman living alone in the North, alone among strangers, it is the sound of North Carolina, the black North Carolina that raised me, that carries me back to a safer place. It is the look and the sound of those men and women — men and women much like my cousins or parents, my aunts and uncles — that root me and hold me safe. And when one of them asks me that question — "Where're your people from?" — I smile, for I know the speaker sees me as kin, and that we will both call out towns and names and schools and clubs until we find that one connection that has meaning for us both.

I am in my thirties, in a drugstore in Washington, D.C. The pharmacist takes the prescription form from my hand, hesitates, then decides to go ahead and say it: "Your face sure does look familiar. Where're your people from?" I start the list: "Well, we're all from North Carolina. My mother's

people are from Winston-Salem and Tobaccoville. Their
name is Scales. And my father's people are from Salisbury
and Asheville and Monroe. They're the Trents." We tried
out names and places for a few minutes. Then he looked
closely at me one more time, assessed my age. "Trent . . .
Trent . . . That name rings a bell. Did any of your people
teach school?" "Well, sure," I replied. "There's my aunt Estelle and my aunt Altona — " He cut me off, excited. "That's
it! I knew it! Your aunt Estelle taught me in the third grade
when we lived in Greensboro. You sure do favor her." We
both smiled at the link we had found — two strangers up
north, people who would likely never see each other again,
but connected by family and by place.

It happened most recently just last year. I was attending a
professional conference in another city, where, as is common, the black members of that group got together to catch
up on news and to find and create connections to embrace
us, make us safe. A group of us went to dinner at a restaurant, where I discovered that a colleague sitting across the
table was also from North Carolina. "Where're your people
from?" I asked. And we discovered that his people are from
Winston-Salem, as are mine; and that they lived on Fourteenth Street, which is where my grandparents lived and
where I spent my childhood summers; and that his grandmother's church was Mount Pleasant, where my uncle was
pastor. "What?" he exclaimed. "You're Reverend Crawford's niece?" We were astonished and delighted, and I
started to call him "cousin." We were kin.

This question "Where're your people from?" is a question
I love, because I know it means that I am looking for connections with someone who wants to find connections with
me. It is also a question that is easy to answer. It is a question that makes sense.

It is also how I understand the question of ethnicity. On
the face of it, the question "What is your ethnicity?" is one
of those clear, simple questions like "How old are you?"
"What color are your eyes?" "Where is your house?" It is

asking the question "Where do your people come from?" And we all have an ethnic identity, even though it may not be one that we can define with precision. It may be only faint harkings, vague memories, wistful longings. But everybody's family came from someplace else. We weren't just planted here in Buffalo or Akron or Des Moines some two millennia ago. We are all "ethnics."

It is also the only way it makes sense to think about the question of race. To the extent that it ever made any sense at all, the question "What's your race?" must have meant "Where're your people from?" For it is very likely that at a certain time long ago, back when people traveled slowly, very slowly, across rivers, over mountain chains, through deserts, people from a certain part of the world shared the same gene pool. It is likely that they shared many physical traits. At that time it probably made some kind of sense to think that if a person had certain physical characteristics it meant that that person was from a certain part of the world, and shared many cultural attributes with others who lived in that region. "Ethnicity" names the place, and "race" names how you are supposed to look, and perhaps act, based on that point of origin. Thus, the answer to the question "Where're your people from?" would have also been the answer to questions of race or ethnicity. Indeed, it would have made those questions irrelevant.

But now that people move around the globe quickly and easily, settling and starting families anywhere and with anyone, questions of race and ethnicity become more confused. Now, at the end of the twentieth century, there are generations and generations of white Africans and black Germans and blond Navajos. The Olympic star skating for the United States is named Yamaguchi, and the star who represents France has dark skin and African features.

Despite this confusion—or perhaps because of it—we hold tenaciously to rigid notions of race and ethnicity, pouring new meaning into these terms. Today, here in America, "race" and "ethnicity" are clumsy codes for other kinds of meaning. They have come to mark the degree of acceptance, the degree of difference. They show how many standard deviations you are from the norm.

Think of the people who live in Tunisia, Algeria, Morocco. Americans would probably consider them a distinct ethnic group: these are people from North Africa, the Maghreb — interesting people, different people. But this is not the French view. The French see them as a different "race." They look at them with disdain, those people whose countries they looted and pillaged, people they maimed, raped, and killed. They mutter in French, with contempt, "*Sale race!*" — "Dirty race! Dirty people!" For if Algerians are sufficiently Other, then it doesn't matter what the French did to them. To Americans, who are not intimately involved with oppressing them, they are simply people from another part of the world, an ethnic group. But to the French, who must work hard to see them as Other, not quite human, they are a race. It is the same group, but a different relationship of power. We are talking about the same people, but the terms used — "ethnic group" or "race" — describe the distance between the speaker and the group, and the complexity of their connection. Similarly, here in America, the earliest Italian immigrants who lived in the South were sent to the Negro schools. They were so "different" to white Southerners that they were thought to be a different racial group. Now, of course, less than a hundred years later, Italian Americans have assimilated to the point that they are considered an "ethnic group."

Historian John Hope Franklin thinks of "ethnicity" as "a way station, a temporary resting place for Europeans as they become American." But even this temporary resting place is denied black Americans. We are still members of a race, not an ethnic group. Thus, when black Americans suggest replacing the term "black" with the term "African American," it is more than a word game. It is about moving our group definition — and hence ourselves — from a racial group to an ethnic group. It is about wanting to become a more integral part of the American community, to move closer to the norm.

But how helpful is that new phrase? Does the term "African American" have the same meaning as "Polish American"? We immediately see one poignant difference, for the term "African American" refers to a huge continent, a continent filled with hundreds of different groups of people who speak hundreds of different languages — groups with different ways of working and defining kinship and raising babies and organizing celebrations. We can only refer back to a continent, not knowing which of those many different groups was home to our ancestors. We have a vague, undifferentiated "there," a sense of longing for that unknown "then." But how does that vague there and then blend with this America today for African Americans?

I think about the black ice-hockey player skating onto the ice, getting ready for the big game. Suddenly he hears the organist announce his arrival on the ice by playing the organist's version of African jungle music. It happens everywhere the team plays, in rink after rink, city after city. "It's unnerving," he told a newspaper reporter. "I never get to be just another member of the team. The music always announces me as that black player, the one whose people came from somewhere in Africa." He didn't say more, but my guess is that the organist doesn't play a specific tune when a player whose people came from England or Czechoslovakia or Finland or Poland skates onto the ice. And why should he? Those are just regular guys. It's that black hockey player who is different. He's the one who comes *from* somewhere else, while the others *are* somewhere. They are here. They are Americans. But the black team member is not here in the same way, even though it is more than likely that his ancestors have been in this country hundreds of years longer than the ancestors of the Polish American player. Some become American, while others are perpetual immigrants, and it has little to do with how long ago your ancestors came here from someplace else. Some get to move into the here and the now, while others are pushed back again and again into the then and the there. Jungle music at the ice rink in Boston, 1990.

Some give up. After trying for hundreds of years to catch hold of the "American" part of "African American," some decide to accept the definition "Other," to celebrate it and raise that celebration to high art. I am reminded of the talk a black college administrator gave to high school students some years ago, where she discussed why they should go to college and what they might experience there. "You will have a hard time in college," she explained, "because there is a lot of writing required at this school, and black people are not used to writing. We come from an oral African tradition." I was dumbfounded. I immediately thought of all of the wonderful writers and scholars from Africa and the African diaspora — Wole Soyinka and Chinua Achebe, Buchi Emecheta and Leopold Senghor. And what about Jamaica Kincaid and Derek Wolcott, John Hope Franklin and John Edgar Weideman and Rita Dove? Not used to writing?! And I thought of the criminally poor schooling that so many black students receive. Why let white America off the hook for what it has done to their life chances?

The more I thought about her statement, the more curious it became. If she believed that there was some bizarre genetic connection between being from Africa and not being able to write well, what should we make of the fact that she, a light-skinned black person, must have had some ancestors from Europe? Did that mean that she, as well as the light-skinned students in that room, carried the writing code on their European genes, whereas the students with dark skin carried only drums on their African genes? And if so, were some of the black students therefore more likely to be better writers than others?

But what confused me most about that statement was that it seems to ignore the fact that African Americans have been in this English-speaking land for more than four hundred years now, and that people who live near one another learn each other's ways. This language, English, should pretty much be ours by now. And the ability to write English should belong to us as much as it belongs to the second-generation Czech student whose grandparents were probably peasant farmers who never learned to read. Do Czech families also glory in their "oral tradition"? Or do they push their children hard to learn this new language so they can make something of themselves in this, their new home? If an African woman from Songhay moved her family to Mali, would she expect that some four hundred years later her family would not be fluent in the language of that country? What is normal is for those who go to a new place to learn the ways and the language of that place. What is normal is for the language and ways of the place we left to get mixed up with the new culture. What is normal is for the old ways to grow fainter and fainter, as the ways of the here and now take hold. We are bilingual for a time, and then the old language is lost. We remember a few phrases, a few dishes for family celebrations. But what is normal is to let go, to be allowed to let go of the There.

We all came from somewhere else. We are all "ethnics." But how is the blend made, and what kind of blend is allowed? The blend "Irish American" is not the same as the blend "African American."

Wading through notions of race and ethnicity is like wading through a muddy swamp. Once I finally figure it out in one context, it slips out of my hand in another. I am like Alice in Wonderland, trying to catch one of the slithery "slithy toves."

I try once more.

"Ethnicity." "Where're your people from?" One person answered: "My mother is from France, my father, from England." Someone said he looked as if he might have ancestors from Italy. He was scornful. "Certainly not! Not Italy, of all places." But really, how could he know? To this man, the life of his family began in France and England several hundred years ago. To him, there was nothing before his collective family memory. He is comfortable answering that question because he is comfortable knowing so little. But certainly his mother's people lived somewhere else before they moved to France. Perhaps Morocco, perhaps Spain. Perhaps even Italy. And where did his father's family travel from? This is a hard question to answer, for, like you and me, he has had hundreds of thousands of ancestors over the past several millennia and knows next to nothing about them. One thing we do know, however, is that his ancestors traveled through many other parts of the world on their long, long trek from Africa. For isn't it true that life started in Africa and spread around the world from there? And aren't we all just variations on an African theme?

I think the difficulty in understanding the notion of ethnicity comes from asking the wrong question all along. The question should not be "Where did your people come from?" but rather "What countries did your people travel through on their way here from Africa?" Or maybe "What was the most recent stop your people made on their trek to this place from Africa? Was it Denmark? Turkey? Bolivia? Vietnam?"

I add one final complication to a very clear question. Remember that the American rule of racial purity states that Americans who can trace any ancestry back to Africa are black, African American. Then remember that all the people in this country started out on their journey to America from Africa. The result is startling, but cannot be escaped. Those Americans who call themselves white are all pretending to be something else — "passing." But they deny her to no avail. For Mother Africa is mother to us all. And we are all African Americans.

An Ordinary Day

The walls they build to separate us really work. If we cross over them, we risk rejection, which reminds us that it is safer to stay in our place. It takes a lot of courage to ignore those barriers — to climb over them, or to reach out and invite someone into our world. Sometimes I can find that courage, and sometimes I can't. Here is one example.

When my friends have babies, I like to buy books for the newborn. I like to start the library for yet one more book-lover in the world! For a long time, my favorite new baby gift was Goodnight, Moon, *a simple and beautiful book that my son loved as a child and that soothes me to this day. More recently, I have been giving copies of* The Enchanted Hair Tale, *a story about a little black boy who is teased because he wears his hair in dreadlocks. It is a gentle book — one of those books where you can't tell which is more lovely, the text or the pictures.*

But just recently, as I was about to buy this book for a new baby, I hesitated—for I was planning to give it to people who were not-quite-yet good friends and who are not African American. All of a sudden I was anxious. I was not sure how they would respond to the gift of a book that was, to me, so very personal—a gift from inside my culture, across the wall, to them, in their culture. Would they be able to see the beauty and the love? Would they understand that the story could illuminate their lives too? Or would they be embarrassed to receive a book about a black child, see only stigma, devalue the book as we black Americans are devalued?

Sometimes you have to take a leap of faith. Sometimes you just have to remember that either they will appreciate this gift of your culture, and it will enrich your friendship, or they will not, and you will be able to bear the rejection. But it takes courage to do this. And sometimes I have it, sometimes I don't.

This last essay is about a day I spent with one of my former students, Michael Campbell, a member of the Iroquois Cayuga Tribe, Turtle Clan. This time it was Michael who reached out across the barriers that separate us to invite me into his world and to introduce me to the richness and complexities of his culture. I don't know if it was difficult for him to invite me to his home that day. But I do know that his gift made my life richer. For this was a day in which I discovered—once again—how wonderfully we are all different, and how blessedly much we are all the same.

Corline and Michael laughed when I said that, if asked what I did during the Christmas holidays, I would say I had spent a day in Gowanda—Gowanda, population 2,906, a small town one hour south of Buffalo. But it was a day worth talking about, a day to write about. A day so rich, so full of surprises, that I still have not understood it all. Let me tell you about that day. Perhaps in the telling, its meaning will become clear to me.

It all began in a class on constitutional law. In order to

present the freedom-of-religion issue in a meaningful way, I had assigned the Indian religion cases, as well as an essay on Indian religion from Paula Gunn Allen's book *The Sacred Hoop*. John Mohawk, a professor of Native American studies, came to provide his interpretation of those cases. It was during that class that Michael spoke for the first time. He told us that he was a Cayuga Indian. And he told us his understanding of how the U.S. Constitution works for Indians: If land is involved, the white man always wins; if land is not involved, sometimes the Indians get to win. The students were engaged; the discussion was rich. After class, Michael and I talked more about these issues. At the end of our conversation, he asked if I would like to visit the reservation near his home. Startled but pleased, I said yes. We made plans for the visit to take place during the Christmas break. I was to arrive before noon, in time for lunch.

The visit was set for early January. It had snowed in the Southtowns that week. As I waded through the drifts to Michael's home, the snow sifted over the top of my boots. I carried a pot of anemones — bright pink, dark green, against the snow. My first surprise was Michael's home. I knew he lived in a trailer near his parents' house. What I did not know was that his trailer home would be a real home, a home filled with plants, rugs, a grand piano, comfortable furniture, and treasures — Indian art handed down through his family. Michael showed me baskets made of sweet grass. One basket was a girl's sewing kit made in the early 1900s, probably at an Indian boarding school. He showed me pottery, wooden tools, beaded fabric. He explained the different bead designs of the Eastern Indians and the Western Indians. He told me how his relatives had collected these pieces and handed them down to him. He drew a map of New York State, and showed me the reservations of the tribes of the Iroquois Confederacy. He explained why the Cayugas, although part of the Confederacy, were landless. Then he drew a map of the Cattaraugus Reservation, where we would be going that day.

One long, beautifully carved spear hung over a window.

When I asked him its story, Michael told me he had gotten it while traveling with a college singing group in the South Pacific and Australia. The group, from Brigham Young University, was comprised of Indian, Polynesian, and latino students. They had also given concerts throughout Europe. "Can you imagine how wonderful it was to be in other countries," Michael said, "where we, as Indians, were treated as honored guests, instead of unwanted people?" He sounded wistful, remembering. Michael told me that he and his brothers and sisters all went to Brigham Young. Thus, I learned that the Campbell family was a Mormon family, and that Michael was a musician.

About this time, Corline, Michael's mother, walked over from her home to join us for lunch, which had been simmering on the stove. Lunch was Indian corn soup and Indian cornbread. But saying that says almost nothing to non-Indians, for these were tastes I had never known before. The corn soup was made with hominy, beans, and salt pork. The cornbread had a fine, crumbly texture and a bland nutlike taste. "Put salt on it," they said. It was delicious, and I was not too embarrassed to ask for more. The meal was plain and filling, but that plainness should not mislead. Preparing those two dishes is so time-consuming that younger Indian women no longer make them. I was told that cooking the soup itself is a three-day job. The first step is removing the hull from the dry corn kernels with lye. Michael and Corline had asked an older woman on the reservation to cook our meal.

Lunch was a warm and laughing affair. They told me about Indian ways. We discussed Indian hospitality. We told each other about our families. Corline told me that she was a nurse and that she and her husband ran a construction business. Michael was their oldest child.

After lunch we walked over to the Campbell family home, where Corline was gathering things to take with us in the car, for they had decided that we would visit their Amish friends on the way to the reservation. Corline had saved empty boxes and an old quilt to take. "The Amish use everything," she explained. "Wait until you see how Mary uses these boxes for her quilting squares."

The Campbell home was large and rambling. It was clearly a house where children were important. The living room showed signs of a birthday-party sleepover from the night before. Michael had made pizza and birthday cake for them all. But the house was quiet this afternoon. His father had taken some of the children to a basketball meet at a Mormon center ("stake") north of Buffalo.

As I walked around the house, I was struck by the many pictures of children. In one room, there were a dozen individual portraits of children in a row along two walls. When I asked who the children were, Corline said reprovingly: "Michael, you didn't tell Judy that we adopted eight children?" A dozen smiling children looking down from the wall, eight of them adopted. It was an easy statement of generosity that left me speechless.

I noticed in other pictures that groups of the Campbell children were wearing matching outfits. The clothes didn't look like regular children's wear, but more like show wear— white with red trim, black with silver trim. They explained that theirs is a musical family. All the children are raised with music. Michael, the eldest, gives piano lessons to the younger ones. They sing together, and they organize musical revues, which they take around the country.

They were still gathering things to take on our outing when friends stopped by, Mormon missionaries who had recently arrived at the reservation. They were a tall, smiling couple. We shook hands, and they welcomed me to their community. "Sister Judy."

We climbed into Michael's car at last, bundled up and warm. And we traveled along the snow-covered fields, around bends, up hills, past farmhouses with wooden signs lettered by hand— "QUILTS," "BAKERY." We stopped at one of these large houses, parked near a wooden fence. Corline opened the door at the first level ("No bell," she explained). As we walked past stacked firewood, she called out our arrival. John greeted us at the top of the stairs and welcomed us. We took off our boots along with our coats and gloves, so as not to drip snow onto the wooden floor. Mary joined us. Then we all went to the main room to visit.

When I think of that day in Gowanda, the visit in that room is what I first see. A potbellied stove, windows open to trees and fields blanketed by snow. A sewing machine with treadle. Rocking chairs. John and Mary, an elderly Amish couple, both in Amish black—he with a long, flowing white beard; Mary's white hair pulled back in a bun, her organdy cap sitting lightly on a table. Well-worn wooden floors, gleaming from years of life and care. They were a laughing, warm couple, delighted to see Michael and Corline, delighted to have company. Would we have tea? A sweet? John brought out his favorite candy from a cupboard and shared it with us. Wasn't that good? They were also delighted to have a new person to tell their stories to. I heard about their fifteen children. They made me guess how many grand-children they had, and enjoyed my astonishment when they finally had to tell me that it was well over a hundred. They talked about how they met, when they were married. John joked that he had married an older woman! And they chat-ted with Corline and Michael about friends and neighbors they both knew, about visits from long ago.

After a while another Amish figure—black clothes, long gray beard—walked slowly through the snow toward their home. He came in to join us, took a cup of tea, sat in a rocking chair, and rocked. He didn't join the conversation, but rocked and smiled, looking all the while at the ceiling. John explained that his neighbor "wasn't quite right," and that he often came by to visit. What else was he going to do with his days? The man continued to rock and to smile— gently, peacefully. John continued, "Once I asked him why he was always looking up, and he answered that he was counting the stars." "Counting the stars," I thought. "There are worse ways to go through life than sitting with friends and counting the stars."

Mary brought out her quilting pieces to show us—small,

precisely cut triangles and rectangles stored in one of the flat boxes a friend had brought her earlier. She had used string to make a handle for the box lid. Everything was tidy and in its place. She showed us potholders she had pieced together to sell — navy and sky-blue squares angled within a blue-and-white polka-dot border then framed within a light-blue border; peach and light-green print triangles, swirling within a dark-green-and-white polka-dot border. Invisible stitches. She was proud of her work.

Finally, it was time to go. We went back to the kitchen area to put on our coats and boots. John headed for the pantry. There was one more thing we had to taste: sweetened evaporated milk cooked in its can. Like Mexican fried milk, it looked like caramel candy and was twice as sweet. "Too rich, too much," we protested. And we stood there in the kitchen eating it like babies, as he spooned the sweetness out of the can for us. Finally, we waved good-bye, and left.

By then it was late afternoon, and we headed for the Cattaraugus Indian Reservation, about fifteen miles long and ten miles wide, its western border touching the eastern shore of Lake Erie. The sky was turning gray. As we rode into the reservation, I looked for something different. But I don't think I would have noticed anything different at all had it not been for the explanations and descriptions of Michael and Corline. They showed me where Corline's mother lived, where friends lived. Michael pointed out where he had run and played as a child. I noticed there were a lot of trailers on the reservation, a lot of small houses, some poorly maintained. They explained that Indians do not put a lot of money into their houses because they are unable to get mortgages for their purchase. Banks are unwilling to lend money secured by property to which they may not have access (the tribe determines who may come on its land), especially when they cannot control the disposition of that property (the tribe must approve all land sales). They also showed me the new tribal center and library built with money the state gave the tribe when the state took their land for a dam project.

"Less and less land," they noted sadly, angrily. I saw the old brick building that used to be a boarding school for Indian children. Corline's mother had attended that school. The visit to the reservation was a visit to a poor, rural land, a land with too few resources for its people.

Corline told me I would be able to tell when they left the reservation because the streets would get better. She was right. By now it was dark, but Corline and Michael conferred privately, and announced that we had one more stop to make. They would not tell me where we were going. We drove through the streets of Gowanda, through a residential section, and stopped in front of an ordinary looking house. We walked to the side door, which Michael opened with a key. The hallway was paneled. On the wall were framed pictures of singing stars. One of them said "To Michael, with appreciation . . . Marilyn McCoo." "What are these?" I gasped. "What does this mean?" "I used to sing professionally," he explained. At the end of the hall, he opened another door, went to a bank of light switches, and turned them on. We were in another room, another world. It was perhaps two stories high, glass on two sides floor to ceiling. There were plants everywhere, a fountain in the center. The room was dominated by a baby grand piano. And there was yet another piano. And an organ. It was a music room. A breathtaking music room. We walked down several steps into the room, and Michael walked over to the baby grand, sat down and started to play. It was something dramatic — runs and trills, diminuendos and crescendos. Music overflowed the piano and filled the room. I sat there in my snow jacket and wet boots in this magical music room and could not believe the wonder of it all.

We left after a few minutes. Michael refused to play more, perhaps embarrassed. He gave piano lessons in town, and rented this room for the lessons. We got back into the car, and again they took me to an unknown destination. But by the time we got out of the car in downtown Gowanda and stood in front of the restaurant, I had figured it out — dinner!

We ate chicken wings and salad as we talked about the day. They introduced me to friends and neighbors who were there. And it was there that I told them that if anyone asked me what wonderful thing I had done over the holiday, I would answer that I had spent a day in Gowanda, an amazing day, a day like no one else would ever spend. And they laughed — pleased, I think.

We were all exhausted. Michael drove back to their home, where my car was parked. I was introduced to Monty — Corline's husband, Michael's father, who had returned from the basketball meet. I also met some of the other children. The youngest, Charity, was asked to play a piece on the piano for me, and did so with pleasure. They invited me to return for Michael's graduation party, and waved good-bye with warmth and smiles.

It was a long, quiet drive back to Buffalo. As I was driving through the dark, I tried to absorb all that I had seen and eaten and touched and heard throughout the day. It was like that sweetened milk John gave us: too rich, too much to eat at once. And I must tell you, it is now more than eight months from that day, and I still have not absorbed it all.

Part of its importance is the extraordinary kindness and generosity of Michael and Corline. I do not know if that is the Indian way or the Campbell way. But it was a gift of extraordinary dimension, for they opened up to me their life as a family, as a people, as friends and neighbors, as members of a religious community.

The day also makes me think of those wooden Russian dolls — the ones you open only to find that there is another doll inside it, which, when opened, contains yet another small doll. Treasure inside treasure. What was different about this day, however, was that each treasure was different. They were not all the same doll, different sizes. It was as if there were first a glimpse of a deer, within that, a poem, and within that, the smell of a baby's skin. Treasure within treasure.

And there was also something about that day that made

me think about how we do not know one another. We do not know our neighbors; we do not know the students in our classes; we do not know the people we see every day. I had never broken bread with the Cayuga, laughed with the Amish, been called "Sister" by Mormons. But how easy it was to know them. And they live only an hour's drive away.

What is still hard for me to understand, however, is that although it was a day of surprises and gifts, it was also an ordinary day. I went visiting and met new friends. We talked and ate and laughed together. And isn't this ordinary? Perhaps not. Perhaps this is really extraordinary all the time. Or perhaps we never stop to think of the gifts of an ordinary day.

Appendix

Teachers in many different disciplines are currently revising traditional academic material in order to address in class the issues discussed in these essays — exclusion and inclusion, sameness and difference, separation and community. They want to make sure their students understand the important contributions that many diverse groups have made to the world. In an earlier essay, I suggested that people who are bilingual and bicultural may be more likely to appreciate and respect the different communities in America. In this essay, I show how I have changed some teaching techniques to help my students become more "bilingual and bicultural" — that is, more connected with the dignity and value that inheres in each of these communities. I also address why I think it is important that law students possess this attribute.

Sameness and Difference in a Law School Classroom: Working at the Crossroads

Introduction

I was recently invited to be on a panel that would discuss teaching law students about difference. How we deal with people we consider "different" is an important issue, and I was pleased to participate. But something about the formulation of the issue troubled me, for it seems to me that "difference" is all that our students know, all that most of us know. If we teach only about difference, we teach nothing new: we merely reinforce the categories that separate us. One member of the audience suggested that one might teach about difference in the classroom by inviting black students to the front of the room to give a presentation to the white students on "what it is like to be black." There might be some value in this — some white students might learn something new. But much of it would be wrong. The physical separation itself speaks powerfully. I imagine that the black students would express rage and sadness, and that the white students would feel guilt, anxiety, and pity. This way of teaching would only solidify the categories "black" and "white." The wall separating the students would grow higher and higher.

After struggling with this formulation for some time, I have concluded that it is valuable to teach about difference only if we teach about sameness at the same time. It is valuable only if we teach the students to see the connectedness between people where they formerly saw only disconnectedness. And only if they see the difference as important and valuable will they want to connect themselves with that difference and become a part of it. We must teach them to see difference with respect, thus encouraging them to find the sameness. We must help them blur the categories, turn concrete walls to powder.

In order to achieve this, I encourage students to enter a world they see as different. I try to show them that world in a way that is compelling and enticing. I try to show the richness and value of that world in order to encourage them to enter it in a positive way. I try not to add feelings of guilt or alienation, but rather to engender feelings of community.

This is what I call "working at the crossroads." It is a concept that is familiar to me because I live at the crossroads, and living there has enlarged my vision. I have written about my struggle to come to terms with being a white black woman, my struggle to live at this particular crossroads. I have come to see this struggle in revolutionary terms, as a struggle that can create a new way to embrace the world. In her book *Borderlands / La Frontera*, Gloria Anzaldúa describes the result of her struggle to put together the Indian, Mexican, and Anglo cultures that have formed her. She describes the creation of a new consciousness, "a mestiza consciousness," in this way:

> The new mestiza copes by developing a tolerance for contradictions, a tolerance for ambiguity. She learns

to be an Indian in Mexican culture, to be Mexican from an Anglo point of view. She learns to juggle cultures. She has a plural personality, she operates in a pluralistic mode — nothing is thrust out, . . . nothing rejected, nothing abandoned. Not only does she sustain contradictions, she turns the ambivalence into something else. . . .

That focal point or fulcrum, that juncture where the mestiza stands, is where phenomena tend to collide. It is where the possibility of uniting all that is separate occurs. This assembly is not one where severed or separated pieces merely come together. Nor is it a balancing of opposing powers. In attempting to work out a synthesis, the self has added a third element which is greater than the sum of its severed parts. That third element is a new consciousness — a mestiza consciousness — and though it is a source of intense pain, its energy comes from continual creative motion that keeps breaking down the unitary aspect of each new paradigm. . . .

Su cuerpo es una bocacalle. La mestiza has gone from being the sacrificial goat to becoming the officiating priestess at the crossroads.

I replace the term "officiating priestess" with the word "teacher," and get to work.

Teaching from the perspective of a civil rights lawyer, I ask myself how much of that work I can do in the classroom, for I want students to learn much more than how to analyze cases and read statutes, I want them to learn much more than how to read and write and think carefully. I want them to understand how the law is implicated in what they see around them every day. Whom does the law favor? Who is disfavored? Are there similarities, differences, between themselves and those who are favored? Disfavored? To the extent that students who are not Asian American can see this society through the eyes of an Asian American, . . . to the extent that a student who is not gay can see the world through the eyes of a gay person, . . . to this extent will they be less able to engage in the oppression that harms so many.

In order to get to this point, the students have to see themselves at the crossroads. They have to see not only the differences between themselves and others but also the sameness. Anzaldúa describes this doubled vision as a healing one: "At some point, on our way to a new consciousness, we will have to leave the opposite bank, the split between two mortal combatants somehow healed so that we are on both shores at once and, at once, see through serpent and eagle eyes." In the classroom I try to create a situation that encourages the students to stand "on both shores at once," to "see through serpent and eagle eyes." I encourage them to see that they, like I, live and work at the crossroads. They can see sameness with, be part of, the black experience and the white experience, the latino experience and the anglo experience, the insider experience and the outsider experience. And they can do it all at the same time.

I use many teaching devices to entice them into worlds they consider "different." I try to have them confront what they are studying directly, personally, either through interviews or fieldwork. If this is not possible, I use proxies for the direct experience — poems, short stories, films, essays, social science material. When I select the material, I ask myself what will engage them so profoundly that they won't be able to escape from it. And if they are able to escape from the power of a poem, perhaps they will be unable to escape from the pictures in a film, or the eyes, tone of voice, in an interview. I try to make it difficult for them to hide, to evade — difficult for them to not see, not understand, not care.

This essay shows how I have used these various techniques in the law school classroom to teach about difference and sameness. First, I describe a seminar that I co-taught on law and social change, for it was during this project that I relearned the importance of these devices to good teaching. Next, I show how I applied the lessons I learned in this seminar to other law school courses — Constitutional Law, Employment Discrimination Law, and a seminar on legal and policy issues affecting women of color. Finally, I assess the value of this teaching method and describe some of the difficulties we all face while working at the crossroads.

Relearning About Learning: A Joint Seminar on Law and Social Change

In the spring of 1987 and 1988 I taught a seminar on law and social change as seen through the process of school desegregation in Buffalo, New York, with Dr. Adeline Levine, a professor of sociology. Having both used the Buffalo desegregation case separately in our respective classes, we decided that bringing our two disciplines to bear on the issue of law and social change in Buffalo would lead to a rich discussion. The focus of the course would be the effect of the judge's school desegregation order on social change in Buffalo: Was the judge successful? Why? Why not? And what does "success" mean in this context? In working together to address these questions, we emphasized the importance of direct student involvement, varied teaching material, joint projects, and community within the classroom.

The students in the course were law students and graduate students in the social sciences. Most were white, some were black. We knew they would be unable to understand the current situation in Buffalo without a solid historical grounding. We also knew that many of the white students would be struggling with their negative stereotypes of blacks, and that many of the black students could see only the cruelty of whites. Thus, the first classes would be crucial. We had to pull the students into the history in a compelling way, one that would force white students to see the passion and struggle of black Americans for an education, and the human consequences of that struggle — one that would push black students to see the powerful support of some white Americans.

For the first class, we had them read slave narratives:

JENNY PROCTOR: ALABAMA

I's hear tell of them good slave days, but I ain't never seen no good times then. My mother's name was Lisa, and when I was a very small child I hear that driver going from cabin to cabin as early as 3 o'clock in the morning, and when he comes to our cabin he say, "Lisa, Lisa, git up from there and git that breakfast." My mother, she was cook, and I don't recollect nothing 'bout my father. If I had any brothers and sisters I didn't know it. We had old ragged huts made out of poles and some of the cracks chinked up with mud and moss and some of them wasn't. We didn't have no good beds, just scaffolds nailed up to the wall out of poles and the old ragged bedding throwed on them. That sure was hard sleeping, but even that feel good to our weary bones after them long hard days' work in the field. I 'tended to the children when I was a little gal and tried to clean the house just like Old Miss tells me to. Then soon as I was ten years old, Old Master, he say, "Git this here nigger to that cotton patch. . . ."

None of us was 'lowed to see a book or try to learn. They say we git smarter than they was if we learn anything, but we slips around and gits hold of that Webster's old blue-back speller and we hides it till 'way in the night and then we lights a little pine torch, and studies that spelling book. We learn it too. I can read some now and write a little too.

—*Jenny Proctor, 87, San Angelo, Texas. Born 1850, in Alabama; slave in Alabama*

IF YOU DO, THEY WILL KILL ME

There was an old white man used to come out and teach Papa to read the Bible.

Papa said, "Ain't you 'fraid they'll kill you if they see you?"

The old man said, "No, they don't know what I'm doing, and don't you tell 'em. If you do, they will kill me."

—*Ellen Cragin, about 80, Little Rock, Arkansas; slave in Mississippi*

They also read Alice Walker's poem "Women":

WOMEN
They were women then
My mamma's generation
Husky of voice — Stout of
Step
With fists as well as
Hands
How they battered down
Doors
And ironed
Starched white
Shirts
How they led
Armies
Headragged Generals
Across mined
Fields
Booby-trapped
Ditches
To discover books
Desks
A place for us
How they knew what we
Must know
Without knowing a page
Of it
Themselves.

It was important that the white students see the fierce and ancient hunger of black Americans for learning. I also wanted them to see how we love and honor those black Americans who came before us and paved our way. For why would one want to find common ground with a people who did not love and respect itself? I wanted them to see our strengths from the first. I also thought it was important for black students to know early on that there have always been white Americans who supported the black struggle for freedom from oppression — the old white man truly risked his life to teach Ellen Cragin's father to read. This was not a class in which black would be recast as supreme goodness and white as supreme evil, for reformulating the categories merely reinforces the notion of barriers; it does not help us be "on both shores at once."

Finally, for this first class, the students read the first six chapters of Richard Kluger's book *Simple Justice*, in which he tells the history of the Supreme Court's decision in *Brown v. Board of Education* through the eyes of the parties involved: the black children and their parents, the lawyers, the judges. The first chapter is about the Rev. Joseph Albert De-Laine, a black South Carolina minister and schoolteacher who sued the white school officials because black children had to walk long, dusty miles to school while white children rode past them in schoolbuses. The first chapter, "Together Let Us Sweetly Live," begins:

> Before it was over, they fired him from the little schoolhouse at which he had taught devotedly for ten years. And they fired his wife and two of his sisters and a niece. And they threatened him with bodily harm. And they sued him on trumped-up charges and convicted him in a kangaroo court and left him with a judgment that denied him credit from any bank. And they burned his house to the ground while the fire department stood around watching the flames consume the night. And they stoned the church at which

he pastored. And fired shotguns at him out of the dark. But he was not Job, and so he fired back and called the police, who did not come and kept not coming. Then he fled, driving north at eighty-five miles an hour over country roads, until he was across the state line. Soon after, they burned his church to the ground and charged him, for having shot back that night, with felonious assault with a deadly weapon, and so he became an official fugitive from justice. In time, the governor of his state announced they would not pursue this minister who had caused all the trouble, and said of him: Good riddance.

All of this happened because he was black and brave. And because others followed when he decided the time had come to lead.

I am quoting extensively from the material assigned for that first class because I hope that you, the reader, are engaged, that you are feeling the power of the story of these lives and that you are thinking that there might be dignity and honor on both shores. For this is the beginning of the work at the crossroads.

In the class for which this reading was assigned, the first substantive class of the semester, we showed *Awakenings: 1954–56,* the first segment of the film series *Eyes on the Prize.* This film portrayed race relations in the South at the time of the 1954 *Brown* decision, through pictures of black children in dilapidated black schools, the trial of the white men accused of murdering fourteen-year-old Emmett Till for whistling at a white woman, and the development of the Montgomery bus boycott.

The first three weeks thus provided historical background. We discussed the *Brown* decisions and the post-*Brown* South, then the move of school desegregation West and North. In order to help the students understand the fierce resistance to integration in America, and as a framework for thinking about how residents in Buffalo might view the impending court order to desegregate, we presented the story of Little Rock, Arkansas, where there was massive state resistance to court-ordered school desegregation. We used both film and primary material, such as excerpts from court orders, proclamations by Governor Faubus and President Eisenhower, and news stories. Thus, the students not only read about the events at Central High School on September 23, 1957 ("A howling, shrieking crowd of men and women outside Central High School, and disorderly students inside, forced the authorities to withdraw eight Negro students from the school today, three and one-half hours after they entered it . . . ,"), they also could see the mob, and the terror of the black students that day. They watched fifteen-year-old Elizabeth Eckford walk alone through the mob to the bus stop, schoolbooks in her arms, and they saw a white woman she didn't know come out of the mob and stand next to her until she was safely on the bus.

They also read an essay by James Baldwin, "A Fly in Buttermilk," in which Baldwin describes his visit with a boy who was the only black student in a newly integrated Southern high school, as well as his meeting with the white principal of that school. With the honesty and clarity of thought for which he is so famous, Baldwin shows us the pain they both confront.

To present the problems of school desegregation in the North, we focused on Boston. We selected Boston for two reasons: first, because Boston is much like Buffalo, a largely working-class Catholic town with sizable, Irish, Italian, and black populations; and second, because the desegregation struggle in Boston took place immediately before the Buffalo struggle and influenced Buffalo's response to the court order to desegregate. To present the Boston story, we assigned the first four chapters of *Common Ground* by Anthony Lukas. In this selection, Lukas introduces the reader to the three families through whose lives he tells the story of the Boston struggle: a black family in Roxbury, a white student at Harvard Law School, and an Irish Catholic family in the projects. Like Baldwin, Lukas presents the lives and concerns of these three families with understanding and respect. Finally, we reached Buffalo's story. The students read how, as long ago as 1840, black parents in Buffalo engaged in non-violent protest and legal action in an effort to get their children admitted to the white city schools.

For the first part of the course, then, we taught the historical background through film, poetry, news clippings, court documents, essays, and personalized historical text. We used this material as proxies for personal involvement.

For the second part of the course, we involved the students directly in the process of school desegregation in Buffalo; no proxy was needed. Instead, we supplemented the court documents and social science literature with class interviews and field trips.

During this part of the semester, major actors in the desegregation case came to our seminar to discuss the litigation and the desegregation of the schools, as well as their role in that process. Thus, the students were able to interview Judge John Curtin, who ordered the desegregation of the Buffalo schools in 1976 and who still had jurisdiction over the case; Eugene Reville, superintendent of the Buffalo public school system during the entire implementation period; Frank Mesiah, a named plaintiff and co-chair of one of the organizational plaintiffs in the case; David Jay, one of plaintiffs' attorneys; and Marilyn Hochfield, an early community activist involved in the litigation and, later, one of plaintiffs' attorneys. The students asked them about this process of social change in Buffalo: What really went on? How did the various communities in Buffalo respond to the court order? What was the personal involvement of these major actors in the process? What in their background made them respond the way they did? What was really going on in the Buffalo schools today? Did the lawsuit really make a difference? What kind of difference? Was it a success? What did they consider "success"?

At the same time that the students were interviewing these

community actors in the classroom, they were studying school desegregation firsthand outside the classroom. Each student was required to spend several hours visiting at least one of the public schools in Buffalo to see what they could learn about the process of integration. They also had to write a report about their visit: Where did they go? What did they see? With whom did they speak? What did they learn? This project particularly engaged the students. Moving out of the classroom into the community gave them a direct and personal involvement with the issues we had been grappling with in class. It also gave them a sense of control over their own research: they would decide which school (or schools) to visit, the time of their visit, and how they would shape the questions they asked. They would decide whether to go alone or with a classmate. Some decided to visit schools they had attended as a child, or schools their children were attending; some visited two schools in order to compare, for example, a magnet school and a nonmagnet school. We provided them with a list of questions to think about during their visits:

> (1) *Is the school integrated?* How is it integrated? Note the racial configuration of classroom, school; note extent of integration in non-structured settings, such as halls, library, lunchroom; (2) *What is going on in the integrated setting?* Does it foster positive relations between majority and minority students? Does it create a good learning situation for minority students? (3) *How does the teacher relate to majority and minority students?* (a) Note, for example, who gets called on more in class, who gets called on for the easy and the hard question; note whether the teacher stands near some students—in a controlling way or in a supportive way; does the teacher wait longer for an answer from some students? (b) Note also the textbooks: are different kinds of people portrayed in the textbooks? How are minorities portrayed? and (4) *Does the physical setting foster a*

good learning situation for minority students? Note
material on bulletin boards, walls; note magazines
and books on display in the library and classrooms.

But it was they who would come back to the classroom with
the raw information we needed so badly if we were to understand the real situation in the Buffalo school system some
twelve years after the court order to desegregate.

The students' contributions to the education of the group
were valuable, and truly needed — the different interviewing
perspectives, their fieldwork, their seminar papers would all
help us understand better the connection between law and
social change in Buffalo. It was also valuable for them to be
in a class where some boundaries were blurred: law and social science, teacher and student, black and white professors,
black and white students. We also used the classroom dynamics, for even as the students were studying integration
and self-segregation within the Buffalo public schools, they
were seating themselves by race within our classroom. We
decided not to comment on this in class, but to change our
seats each class session to see if this would disrupt the pat-
tern of self-segregation. After about five class sessions, the
students felt safe enough to notice and comment on the self-
segregation, which was perceived by the white students as
"the black students sitting together," instead of "the white
students sitting together." The black students maintained
that they sat together because they had known each other a
long time and pointed out that the law students, who also
knew each other, took seats together. After this discussion,
there was more self-integration within the classroom, in part
because they were more self-conscious about the issue, and
partly because the white and black students began to know
each other better and to have more things to say to each
other.

My hope is that their professors' ability to work comfortably at the crossroads helped them see this as a possibility for
themselves. I also hope that they learned from our struggle
and our failures. During one class, I was particularly aggra-

vated by what I considered racist comments by a white student and responded sharply to her. After class, I discussed the incident with Professor Levine. I thought I should have been more patient with the student's comments — indeed, she was in class precisely because there were things she did not know. What should I do to address the incident? Professor Levine suggested that I think of a way to use the incident as part of the work of the seminar. Therefore, at the beginning of the next class, after apologizing to the student, I pointed out to them all how difficult it was to address the issues of race even in that classroom, where black and white chose to come together in a protected environment to discuss these troubling matters. How much harder must it have been, then, for white and black parents in Buffalo to change their ways of thinking and acting not because they chose to but because one judge had told them to do it. Hopefully, exploring my struggle helped them understand the struggle of others with more generosity.

I hope the students were able to be engaged in the school desegregation struggle in a positive way, and to see the important roles played by both black and white Americans in that struggle. I hope that the white students learned to view black culture and history as rich and compelling, worthy of respect, a shore on which it might be possible to stand. And I hope that the black students were able to see the very real anguish and courage of some white Americans with respect to racial issues in this country. If the students were not yet comfortable on both shores at once, perhaps they had stood there for an instant. And perhaps they at least knew this was possible.

Applying the Lessons Learned

During this joint teaching project, I relearned the importance of direct student involvement, varied teaching material, and community within the classroom. I discovered how to use diverse forms of written material to teach about the richness and value of other cultures, and how to use interviews and fieldwork to engage them more fully in the lives and issues of others. I also learned to weave these lessons on sameness and difference into a law school course that addressed substantive sociological, historical, and legal issues. Since that time, I have tried to apply some of these techniques to my other law school classes. In the next section, I discuss the application of these methods to three courses: Constitutional Law II (First Amendment), Employment Discrimination Law, and a seminar on legal and policy issues affecting women of color.

Course: First Amendment

In this course, we study issues involving freedom of speech and freedom of religion. I give an example from each area to show how I use these techniques to engage the students directly with the issue, and to push them toward recognizing and valuing sameness and difference.

Speech

We work with cases such as *Cox v. Louisiana* and *Chicago v. Gregory* to address the issue of when the actions of demonstrators will be protected under the First Amendment and when the state interest in noise abatement or crowd control, for example, will prevail. Both cases involve protests against racial segregation. In *Gregory*, protesters marched to the mayor's home to protest segregated schools; and in *Cox*, 2,000 black students demonstrated in front of a courthouse to protest the jailing of fellow students who had been arrested for picketing stores with segregated lunch counters. I learned early on that this speech issue would be an important area for developing ideas of sameness and difference.

The first year I taught this course, as we were discussing

Cox, I asked the students whether Reverend Cox's exhortation to the black demonstrators to sit in at the lunch counter was protected under the First Amendment. Cox was, I reminded them, urging the demonstrators to violate a state law that required eating establishments to segregate diners by race. I asked the class whether the Constitution protects speech that urges others to violate state statutes. After a long silence, one student said: "You mean, there used to be laws like that?" I was aghast. Could it really be that although I had lived more than half my life under those laws, society was now pretending that those laws had never existed? As a result of this new understanding of what they did not know, what they had not been taught, I modified the course syllabus. During the next class we read and discussed the black laws of Virginia between 1866 and 1922. What did they tell us about American history? How had they shaped us all? What would be the likely impact of those laws generations later? But this presentation was too abstract to reflect the harsh impact of those laws on my life and on the lives of others. I needed something stronger.

Therefore, the next year, after we discussed the civil rights demonstration cases, I showed the film *Ain't Scared of Your Jails: 1960–61* from the series *Eyes on the Prize.* This film portrays the initial training in nonviolence of black college students who would participate in a sit-in at a segregated luncheonette counter. The law school students also experienced the power of nonviolent protest as they watched white hoodlums pull the students from the counter stools and beat and kick them as the police watched. They also watched the planning for the Freedom Rides, which would protest continued segregation at interstate bus terminals. They saw both white and black college students getting ready for the trip, talking about their commitment and their fears. And finally, they watched as the buses were fire-bombed and as the riders were pulled off the bus, beaten, and jailed.

I chose this film in large part because it showed the courage of both black and white college students, as well as their ability to work together. I was hopeful that the students in the class would be able to identify with the demonstrators in part because they were also students, and in part because these students were presented as heroes. Their response was as powerful as the film itself: a stunned silence . . . a few red eyes . . . some students leaving the room halfway through the film . . . a few halting words: "I didn't know. . . ."

Although this film met my goals of engaging the students in a thoughtful way and of getting them to look in a positive way at the roles of both blacks and whites, the last time I taught this course I added fieldwork to the unit on demonstrations. Several of my colleagues have been actively engaged in a Pro-Choice network in Buffalo; others serve as escorts at a local abortion clinic, where they help prospective clients walk through pro-life demonstrators and into the clinic. After listening to their discussions, I realized that it made little sense to simply read or view a film about demonstrations when the students could go and see one for themselves.

One goal of the field visits was to flesh out the written class material so the students could witness for themselves the power of the First Amendment's guarantee. Another goal was to give them the opportunity to do the kind of work lawyers do when they advise their clients at a demonstration. They had already seen that in the demonstration discussed in *Gregory*, the demonstrators were accompanied on their march by their attorney and an assistant city counsel, and the police were accompanied by an assistant city counsel. In the case of the abortion clinic in Buffalo, which of these protest activities would be protected under the First Amendment? Which would not?

I gave them guidelines for their fieldwork. Because abortions are performed at this particular clinic early Saturday mornings, the students were to spend at least one hour observing between 8:00 and 10:00 A.M. I gave them a map of that location and asked them to stand across the street from the pro-life demonstration, which was near the entrance to the clinic. Each was to stand with another student; they were to observe, not participate. If a demonstrator tried to engage them in conversation, they were to move silently to another area or leave. Because the clinic is located on a much traveled city street and next to a post office, I asked them to think about whether the free speech rights of the demonstrators would vary depending on where they were standing— on the post office steps, the sidewalk, the street, the clinic parking lot, the adjacent parking lot of a private business that had granted them access. We discussed the local ordinances that would be involved, ordinances regarding loud noises, harassment, and obstruction of public walkways. I also contacted the director of the clinic before the student visit, to explain our project and to advise her when the students would be coming. We would meet immediately after their observation for a class discussion.

The students were engaged, and excited about exploring how they would advise the demonstrators, their clients. They raised several other issues after this fieldwork. One was the courage of the demonstrators to take such a visible stand for their beliefs. Another was the role of the police at the demonstration: were they as vigilant as they might have been about the constitutional rights of clinic patients to a legal abortion? I pointed out that the police are there with the same demonstrators day after day and that, much like the relationship that grows between police, criminals, and criminal law attorneys, the police and the demonstrators come to know one another. How might this affect the legal rights of those who are outside this relationship?

One of the most important issues we addressed came out of a comparison of the demonstrators in the film they had seen earlier in the week—civil rights activists of the 1960s— and the demonstrators they had personally observed: pro-life activists, with whom they were less sympathetic. How might this affect the legal representation they would offer? Could an attorney truly represent a client whose views he opposed? Could they? Yet wasn't there really a profound sameness between the demonstrators against segregation in the South and the pro-life demonstrators in Buffalo? Could they see and respect the sameness as well as the difference? This theme engaged them deeply. Some were startled at the suggestion, others were irate. The pro-life activists were unsympathetic, "different," one student argued, because they brought their children to the demonstration, thus subjecting them to physical danger. "But didn't Martin Luther King Jr. sometimes take his children on marches with him, to teach them the importance of standing up for their rights?" I asked in return, "How is that different?" They returned to this issue in their written reports. One student pointed out that some of the pro-life picketers were singing a civil rights protest song, "Keep Your Eyes on the Prize," during their demonstration. Another, a student who had been both a pro-choice escort and a demonstrator for animal rights, made the following comment: "As I observed all this, two general thoughts ran through my head. The first, in a nutshell, was 'Why don't these lunatics mind their own business?' and the second, which was very disturbing, was 'Good grief, these people remind me of myself!' "

Religion

The Free Exercise Clause of the First Amendment, like the Free Speech Clause, often addresses issues of outsiders trying to be heard, issues of inclusion and exclusion. At its most basic level, it asks whether the state will be able to understand and respect religious beliefs that are not those of the majority. In the casebook, the stories of inclusion and exclusion are disconnected one from the other, disconnected from real lives. I decided, therefore, to teach the Free Exercise Clause by focusing on one group. I would try to make that group visible, try to show how the constitutional issue being addressed mattered to them. I chose to focus on Indian religion, in large part because Buffalo is located in the middle of the Iroquois Confederacy. Thus, it is not uncommon to hear students at this law school identify themselves as, for example, Tuscarora or Cayuga.

For this class discussion, there were two sets of readings. The first consisted of excerpts from Paula Gunn Allen's book *The Sacred Hoop,* which discusses Indian literature within the context of Indian culture and religion. Allen points out the different concepts that underlie Indian and Western religion. What differences might flow from the fact that Indians tend to view space as spherical, not linear, and view time as cyclical, not sequential? From the fact that Indians do not see nature as separate from humanity and do not separate the material from the spiritual or the natural from the supernatural? In Native American thought, the natural state of existence is wholeness, and the purpose of religious ceremony is to reinforce and restore that wholeness. They learned that it is this "essential sense of unity" that underlies all of traditional American Indian culture, including literature and religion.

Once the students are immersed in the richness and complexity of this culture, they read two U.S. Supreme Court decisions to see whether the complexities they had just discovered were addressed in a respectful and understanding way by the Court. In the first case, *Lyng v. Northwest Indian Cemetery Prospective Association,* the Supreme Court found that the right of the Yurok, Karok, and Tolowa Indians to hold religious ceremonies in their sacred land was not injured, despite a government decision to allow road-building and timber-harvesting on that land, which would destroy the privacy and silence needed for their ceremonies. In the second case, *Employment Division v. Smith,* the Court upheld the state's right to deny unemployment benefits to an Indian worker who was fired for using peyote at a religious ceremony, since the use of peyote was illegal in that state. In a further attempt to help us all see the real impact of these decisions on Native Americans, I invited Professor John Mohawk of the American Studies Department to come to class and present his perspective on those cases.

This gave the students an opportunity to understand in a rich way the impact of the Supreme Court decisions on the lives of Indians. Several students noted that they read the cases very differently after reading the excerpts from *The Sacred Hoop*. They had been pulled into that culture in a way that let them read the cases as an "insider," as a participant in Indian culture. Thus, they were able to respond to the sameness within the difference. Also, it is very likely that they, like I, had never before read material by an Indian scholar on Indian literature, or discussed the legal and cultural complexities of court rulings involving Indian rights with an Indian scholar. Who among us had a Native American university professor? And how might that have affected our ability to understand and respect that culture, our willingness to see the sameness as well as the difference?

Course: Employment Discrimination Law

One would think that working at the crossroads would be easier in this course than in others, as these students are already open to the idea that discrimination against people who appear "different" exists and is unfair. What I have found, however, is that these students, like the rest of us, are often able to see only their issue, not the issues of others. They see the difference, not the sameness. For example, black students are often hostile to women's issues, failing to note that many black people are women and must also face gender issues; white women students often want to focus on gender issues alone, failing to note that some women are Asian and must also address issues of ethnicity. The law, and hence the casebooks, also falls into this trap, by separating out issues, for example, by sex or by age, and by failing to point out that black people can be old, that old people can suffer gender discrimination, and that women can be discriminated against because they are Latinas. I attempt to address the concept of sameness and difference in class by pointing out these convergences as often as possible. For example, when we read the sexual harassment material in the casebook, I provide supplementary information on racial harassment. When we read about pay equity as a theory for attacking gender-based wage discrimination, I provide the research on pay equity as a remedy for race/ethnicity-based wage discrimination. Seeing how the issues of "different" people are the same is an important legal tool, for our legal system is based on the notion that one uses the same analytic framework in situations that are factually different yet theoretically the same. An attorney who cannot make this kind of "leap," an attorney who cannot see this sameness and difference at the same time and make use of it, puts her client at a disadvantage.

Several students dramatically portrayed this in a class assignment. I had given them an article from the local newspaper that told the story of Nadine Wilson, a black woman police officer who had been denied transfer to detective over the past several years. The reporter presented the employment profile of the Buffalo police department broken out by race and ethnicity. It showed that while there were many black police officers at the patrol level, Blacks were significantly underrepresented at the detective level. The reporter also explained how detectives were selected, discussed the problem of low turnover at the detective level, and interviewed several black officers. I asked the students how they would advise Ms. Wilson if she asked them for legal advice: Did she have a strong Title VII claim? Under what theory (or theories)? Did they have enough information to make a sound assessment? What else did they need to know? Upon review of their papers, I was stunned to notice that several of the students had seen this as a gender claim only, even though the only evidence relating to gender discrimination in this two-page report was the statement that all the homicide detectives were white men. The students simply were unable to see that, as a black woman, Ms. Wilson had to confront race discrimination as well as gender discrimination. As a result, they ignored all the evidence relating to race discrimination, even though that might well have been Ms. Wilson's strongest claim.

I have not yet figured out how to have the students in this course do "fieldwork" on the subject of employment discrimination. Could they spend a day observing a workplace to see whether they can spot discrimination? It is often not so easily visible. Nonetheless, fieldwork is such an important tool to help students see and think about what they might not have seen and thought about before, that on the first day of class I ask them to work "in the field" by writing a report describing two examples of employment discrimination they have witnessed in some way. I offer several suggestions. (1) Interview a family member or friend. Was your father forced to retire? Has your sister ever been harassed on the job? (2) Have you yourself seen discrimination in the workplace? Have you personally suffered from discrimination? Have you seen discrimination against your co-workers? (3) Look around you now, today. When you are in the checkout line at the grocery store, or eating at a restaurant, look to see who has which jobs, and which are the higher-paying jobs. How likely is it that this is a random occurrence? I explain that I am not asking them to describe what is legally cognizable as employment discrimination, but what seems so unfair that it should be against the law. I also ask them to note on the report whether I may use the example in class, with identifying data removed. I then distribute these stories at the appropriate time during the semester either to illustrate a particular legal issue or to use as hypothetical cases.

Another technique for getting students to look around — and at themselves — with fresh eyes is to use a pay equity chart. At the end of our work on the Equal Pay Act, I provide an introduction to pay equity by giving them a list of jobs connected to three workplaces: restaurant/hotel, airport, and college/university. This is the restaurant/hotel list:

Manager
Desk clerk
Pool attendant

Coat check person
Shoe shiner
Restaurant host/hostess
Maintenance crew worker
Room cleaner

Assuming hotel has two dining rooms, who serves food in:
1. Breakfast/lunch restaurant
2. Dinner restaurant

I then ask students to note the race/ethnicity and sex of the person who is likely to hold these jobs. After they mark their chart, one by one the students identify who most likely holds a specific job. Generally there is consensus. They know that the lifeguard in the hotel pool is young and white, and that the shoeshine "boy" is old and black. If there is any debate at all, it is whether the young white lifeguard is male or female, or whether the old shoeshine "boy" is black or latino. We then talk about the other workplaces. Why it is that the airport attendants who use a computer to check your bag outside are all black men, while those who use a computer inside to check your bags are generally white men and women. How likely is it that these are random employment decisions? What does this say about our society and our places within it? And what are the implications for the lives of these workers?

Finally, I have found it helpful to show the film *Pregnant but Equal* after we discuss the written material on pregnancy discrimination. This is a film about women factory workers who are trying to get management to obey the mandate of the Pregnancy Discrimination Act. The women talk about how they learned of the existence of the statute, and how they worked to educate each other about their rights with respect to pregnancy. They talk about their difficulties getting help from the union or from management, and note that they had to use various self-help techniques, including contacting the local television station when management tried to

deny benefits to a pregnant woman after the law was en-
acted.

This film provides many important topics for discussion,
including the disjunction between the passage of a civil rights
statute and its enforcement. Seeing how hard some working
women struggle for the right to not be fired when they are
pregnant makes the issue real and important to the students.
This film is also helpful because the women who are working together and taking care of each other are both black
and white, women who have not only seen the sameness in
difference but have also used that sameness as an organizing
tool.

Seminar: Legal and Policy Issues Affecting Women of Color

The aim of this seminar is to identify and explore legal and
policy issues that affect women of color — that is, African
American women, Latinas, Indian women, and Asian American women. Thus, as conceptualized, the entire seminar re-
volves around exploring sameness and difference. Is there a
way in which the issues confronting the various women of
color groups are the same? Different? And how are they the
same or different from the issues facing white women, men
of color, white men? The work of the course was thus centered on the crossroads. I soon discovered that one of my
main tasks during the semester would be to keep the students there, to encourage them not to run back one of the
roads to a safer place, to what they call "home," for the
major issue here, as in the employment discrimination class,
is developing the ability to see the issues of others as one's
own.

We focused on several substantive issues: employment, cit-
izenship, reproduction, and family issues. For most of these
issues, thus for most class sessions, there were readings written by or about women from all four groups. One of the

introductory classes, "Who Are the Different Women of Color? Listening to Our Voices," consisted entirely of literature written by different women of color authors. My hope was that, by reading poetry, essays, and short stories by these women whose lives seemed so different, the students would learn to see the similarities. In fact, that was the result. When they read Mitsuye Yamada's poem "Masks of Woman,"

> This is my daily mask
> daughter, sister
> wife, mother
> poet, teacher
> grandmother.
>
> My mask is control
> concealment
> endurance
> my mask is escape
> from my
> self . . .

black, white, and latino women all marveled: "She could have been writing about me!" In the section on employment, they noted the many similar kinds of work these groups of women have performed over the years in order to support themselves and their families: factory work, prostitution, farm work, domestic service. It was helpful when a white student told us that she had supported herself for many years doing domestic work: this was not only a woman of color issue. An African American student whose mother had immigrated from South Africa and worked in a family-owned restaurant in New York City saw her mother in a new light after reading a Chinese woman's account of working in the family restaurant in Chinatown. And when the students struggled to read the essays by Anzaldúa in which she moves with ease from English to Spanish, "outsider" was redefined as everyone who was not bilingual: the Latinas and Latinos in the class became the ones with privileged knowledge.

This was also a class in which white students were the minority, and students of color were the majority. This became a fruitful area for discussing issues of sameness and difference: How long did it take before the "majority" students began to abuse their power? Before the "minority" students felt silenced? As one might expect, it did not take long. About halfway through the semester, I decided to force this issue and asked the "majority" students to not speak for twenty minutes in order to encourage the "minority" students to speak out. Most of the "majority" students accepted this with good grace, laughing as they recognized the newly inverted power structure within the classroom. However, one woman of color was enraged at being silenced yet again in a law school classroom. Although I still think it was a good idea to call for this break, if only to open a discussion of what was going on in the classroom, her comment reminded me once again that the struggle to create a new kind of community without replicating the faults of the old is not an easy one.

In the last readings for the course, I focused even more directly on the issue of sameness and difference. The introductory material for that class assignment asked: "Who are the different women of color groups? How helpful are those categories? How are we the same? How are we different? Are we too much the same? Too different? Can we transcend our 'sameness' and work together? Can we transcend our 'difference' in order to work together?" For this assignment, they read, among other things, Audre Lorde's troubling essay on anger and hatred among black women, an article comparing chicana and anglo feminism, and my essay on the difficulties of defining and maintaining categories when one is black and constantly mistaken for white. I also included a picture from the book *Black Indians* — a nineteenth-century photograph of an Indian woman in buckskin and long braids, a woman with dark skin and African features. This was the class that provoked the richest and most powerful reflections from the students, as they noted similarities and differences among groups, as they grappled with their own memories of rejecting and being rejected within their own communities, their rejection of women in other groups, and their confusion as definitions and categories change from time to time and from place to place. Because of these constantly shifting identities, our notions of sameness and difference are always in flux.

Conclusion

The only helpful way to teach about difference is to teach about sameness at the same time. Only if our students are able to see others as they see themselves, able to care about the issues of others as they care about their own issues, will they then be able to answer in a generous way "Why does it matter? Why should I care?" Only if we teach sameness at the same time will they see themselves implicated in the answer. They must learn that they can stand—indeed, are standing—on both shores of the river at the same time.

To do this, I try to bring them into worlds that they consider "different"—first by making them feel safe enough in the classroom to take this step, and second by presenting the new world as a place of dignity and respect. My aim is to give them a sense, if only for a fleeting moment, of being on two shores at once. For this is the first and hardest step. Once they know that they can be at more than one place at the same time, it is easier to conceptualize being at three, or four, or five places at the same time. For there are many roads that come together at the crossroads, the roads of ethnicity and color and religion and sex and class and (dis)ability, and many, many more.

This approach to teaching should yield positive results for both the study and the practice of law. First, making the students active participants in the study of law—either through film or interview or fieldwork—validates them as having a place in the "law" and as important in creating and enforcing the "law." This increased sense of their own possibilities as lawyers should inspire greater motivation to learn. For example, when students view the film *Pregnant but Equal*, they hear and see women they might want to represent one day. This, it seems to me, might lend some urgency to their study of the Pregnancy Discrimination Act. Second, it is simply more fun to learn through active participation and with different kinds of material. Also, the use of varied media for teaching might also say to the students that breaking out of a familiar (teaching) mode, trying something "different," is an attribute to be valued, and one that can yield unexpected insights and pleasures. And finally, my guess is that students who find it hard to concentrate in the law school classroom because they feel excluded ("different") will learn better if their values, and the contributions of their culture, are included in the learning experience.

This teaching approach should also improve the way they practice law. For example, this work at the crossroads might lead them to represent clients whom they might earlier have considered unsympathetic ("too different"), because they will be more able to see the sameness. Indeed, because they might have more respect for these clients, they should be better able to hear, understand, and believe their stories; they might be more willing to enter their clients' worlds in order to better develop their cases. Finally, they should be better lawyers, as they will be able to spot issues others miss. For example, an attorney for Equal Rights Advocates, a public interest law firm that focuses on issues affecting women of color, explained that in order to protect the rights of undocumented Asian and latino women workers who are in abusive relationships, they have given workshops on family law to immigration lawyers, and on immigration law to family lawyers. Thus, because these lawyers understand how Asian and latina immigrants are like all women (family violence), and also how they are different from women who are citizens but like men who are not citizens (immigration issue), and because they understand how these two issues intersect in the lives of undocumented women, they were able to better protect their clients.

It is difficult to assess the success of this teaching approach, for the results will not show up on an exam grade or through the financial rewards of a law career. Success will come only if, at some later time, a flash of memory about something that went on in the classroom illuminates something in the lives of one of these students and leads that student to a broad and generous understanding.

It is also difficult to achieve success. There are powerful limits on what a teacher can do in one semester, meeting once or twice a week, especially since everything else in our society reifies these categories, tells us to stand in one place, and stay there. And there is resistance from the students. Those with privilege don't want to see sameness with those who are denied privilege: Why forge an alliance with those who have less than you? Why weaken and demean yourself in this way? For how can you retain privilege once you truly understand that you are also on the other shore of the river? As the novelist Chinua Achebe explains, "Privilege . . . spreads a thick layer of adipose tissue over our sensitivity." Also, those who are denied privilege often do not want to see sameness with those who have privilege. Why should black students see that there can be honor and dignity in the white world when they know they will be rejected by that world as soon as they try to enter? Indeed, I have my own problem with this. I wonder if it isn't counterproductive for me to encourage black students to temper their rage at white America. Don't they need this rage in order to survive?

It is also difficult to achieve success because the crossroads is a difficult place to be. It is difficult, first of all, because decision-making from that vantage point is very troublesome. One cannot make decisions based on the categories of the parties, on the notion that you are female and that the "other side" is male, once you recognize you are standing on the "other side" too. Standing at the crossroads means, for example, that in a case of court-ordered promotions for black workers formerly excluded from upper-level jobs, one will understand not only the anger of the black workers, their hunger to show what they can do, and their desire to provide more security for their families, but also the concerns of the white workers who fear uncertainty, change, displacement. It means that one will not only appreciate the claims of the Indians who want to maintain their sacred land for religious purposes, but will also appreciate the concerns of the loggers who fear that the lumber mill will close down if they can't cut timber, who fear that they may lose their livelihood, have to uproot their family, lose their home. Thus, if I am "successful" at my work at the crossroads, it does not mean the students will make the decision I might want them to make. It only means that the decision-making process will be more thoughtful, more inclusive, more problematic.

The crossroads is also a difficult place to be in a society like ours, which is defined by internecine warfare. We pit women against men, the able-bodied against the disabled; we create ethnic, racial, and religious groups, and set them to fight. Because we are in a constant state of war, there is enormous pressure to choose up sides, to pledge allegiance to one side or the other. It is politically unpopular to be on both shores at once when there are opposing armies on each shore. It is also disorienting. A white student with close ties to the black community explained in a compelling way the dislocation that takes place when one stands on two shores at once:

> I always challenge white people when they make racist comments in my presence. I cannot be an accomplice to their racism by being silent. This makes me uncomfortable with certain groups of people because I know it is only a matter of time before an offensive remark will be made, and that marks the end of the possibility of an amicable relationship. In this way I feel like an inside outsider . . . or an outside insider.

The work at the crossroads is hard work. As Gloria Anzaldúa reminds us, this "new consciousness — a mestiza consciousness — " although a source of energy and creativity, is also "a source of intense pain."

It is abundantly clear, therefore, why so few people work at the crossroads, or even acknowledge that they are standing there: it is unpopular, it is disorienting, it makes decision-making even more troublesome. Nonetheless, for better or worse, because I live at the crossroads, this is the only way I can teach. I don't always meet my own goals. I have my own problems with sameness and difference. The best I can do is show the students that it can be done, and that it can open up the world.

Notes

A few names and places have been changed for reasons of privacy.

Introduction

Page 3

"such formal, written laws existed in America. . . ." See, for example, Virginia's 1662 law on miscegenation and Louisiana's racial classification statute, repealed in 1983 (F. James Davis, *Who Is Black? One Nation's Definition* [University Park, Pa.: The Pennsylvania State University Press, 1991], 9, 33). The federal government still maintains standards for determining racial identity. On June 9, 1994, the Office of Management and Budget (OMB) announced that it was undertaking a review of the adequacy of these standards. See OMB, "Standards for the Classification of Federal Data on Race and Ethnicity," *Federal Register,* June 9, 1994, vol. 59, no. 110, p. 29831.

"Virginia's 1924 law. . . ." Jane Purcell Guild, *Black Laws of Virginia* (New York: Negro Universities Press, 1936), 35.

"by 1662 the state of Virginia. . . ." Davis, *Who Is Black?* 33.

Page 4

"one drop of black 'blood.' . . ." Ibid.

"the one black ancestor rule. . . ." Ibid., 5.

"This rule applies only to African Americans. . . ." Ibid., 12–13.

"laws, however, were not uniform." See, in general, ibid., chap. 3; A. Leon Higginbotham Jr. and Barbara K. Kopytoff, "Racial Purity and Interracial Sex in the Law of Colonial and Antebellum Virginia," *Georgetown Law Journal* 77 (1989): 1978 (on the 1785 change in Virginia's legal definition of "mulatto").

"Nonetheless, . . . the 'one-drop rule' of racial purity is generally accepted. . . ." Davis, *Who Is Black?* 80.

Page 5
"ownership of African women. . . ." Ibid., 38–39.

"One result of this move. . . ." Ibid., 39–40.

Page 6
"light-skinned black elite. . . ." Ibid., 39.

"legal system formalized this tripartite scheme. . . ." Ibid., 33–37.

"Africans were 'natural slaves. . . .'" Ibid., 41–42.

"Black Pride movement. . . ." Ibid., 77–80.

Commonalities

Page 11
"the status of black women in the law. . . ." See, for example, my article "Black Women and the Constitution: Finding Our Place, Asserting Our Rights," *Harvard Civil Rights–Civil Liberties Law Review* 24 (1989): 9.

Page 19
"some dreams. . . ." Lucille Clifton, *good woman: poems and a memoir, 1969–1980* (Brockport, N.Y.: BOA Editions, 1987), 155.

Page 20

"*Black Rage.*" William H. Grier and Price M. Cobbs, *Black Rage* (New York: Basic Books, 1968).

"*Proud Shoes.*" Pauli Murray, *Proud Shoes: The Story of an American Family* (New York: Harper, 1956).

"*New People.*" Joel Williamson, *New People: Miscegenation and Mulattoes in the United States* (New York: The Free Press, 1980).

Page 21

"But I am not tragically colored. . . ." Zora Neale Hurston, *I Love Myself When I Am Laughing* . . . (Old Westbury, N.Y.: Feminist Press, 1979), 153.

Page 23

"At my father's wake. . . ." Janet Campbell, "Desmet, Idaho, March 1969," in *The Third Woman: Minority Women Writers of the United States*, ed. Dexter Fisher (Boston: Houghton Mifflin Co., 1980), 107. Also in *Voices of the Rainbow*, ed. Kenneth Rosen (New York: Arcade Publishers, 1993).

Page 26

"She boards the bus. . . ." Laureen Mar, "Chinatown I: Seattle Washington," in *Third Woman*, 522.

Page 29

"transgressed boundaries. . . ." Donna Haraway, "A Manifesto for Cyborgs: Science, Technology, and Socialist Feminism in the 1980s," *Socialist Review* 80 (March–April 1985): 65.

Page 31

"the magic wand. . . ." Patricia Williams, "Alchemical Notes: Reconstructing Ideals from Deconstructed Rights," *Harvard Civil Rights–Civil Liberties Law Review* 22 (1987): 431.

Afterword and Preface

Page 34

"Time, the prophet of wisdom." Jason B. Ellis, "Time Passes" (1990), unpublished poem, quoted by permission of the author, my son.

Pages 35

"I guess it should come. . . ." Personal letters to the author, quoted by permission.

Page 36

"I guess it isn't all their fault. . . ." April Walker, *Cabbages and Kings* (literary journal of Monroe Community College, Rochester, N.Y.), Spring 1983, 26.

Family Pictures

Page 48

"I want to lay in the arms. . . ." Lorna C. Hill, "Just Because," in her *Yalla Bitch* (Buffalo, N.Y.: private publication, 1986), 31.

Choosing Up Sides

Page 61

"She who was part-them. . . ." Michelle Cliff, *Bodies of Water* (New York: Dutton, 1990), 97.

"Mo' Black"

Page 68

"Malcolm X was harassed. . . ." Bruce Perry, "Neither White nor Black," *Ethnic Groups* 6 (1985): 292.

Definitions

Page 76
"Lawd! Lawd! I think that is rotten. . . ." John Langston
Gwaltney, *Drylongso: A Self-Portrait of Black America*
(New York: Random House, 1980), 92.

Page 78
"WILL THE REAL BLACK WOMAN. . . ." Audre Lorde,
Sister Outsider (Trumansburg, N.Y.: Crossing Press,
1984), 170.

Marion and Effi

Page 79
This news story appears in *JET*, July 23, 1990, 12–14.

Even Du Bois —

Page 81
"I resented the defensive mechanism . . ." and "I did not
seek contact. . . ." W.E.B. Du Bois, *Writings* (New York:
Library of America, 1986), 628.

Lost Great-Uncle Charles

Page 96
"subverting the racial divide." G. Reginald Daniel, "Pas-
sers and Pluralists: Subverting the Racial Divide," in
Racially Mixed People in America, ed. Maria P. P. Root
(Newbury Park, Calif.: Sage Publications, 1992), 91.

On Being Like a Mule

Page 99
"It is impossible. . . ." James Baldwin, *The Evidence of
Things Not Seen* (New York: St. Martin's/Marek, 1985), 31.

"dictionary. . . ." *The Random House Dictionary of the English Language* (New York: Random House, 1987), 1261.

Page 100
"de mule uh de world. . . ." Zora Neale Hurston, *Their Eyes Were Watching God* (Urbana: University of Illinois Press, 1937), 20.

(Dis)Continuities

Page 107
" 'Girl from Martinique.' " Cliff, *Bodies of Water*, 76.

Page 109
"all margins are dangerous. . . ." Mary Douglas, *Purity and Danger: Analysis of the Concepts of Pollution and Taboo* (London: Ark Paperbacks, 1966), 121.

"when a deformed child is born. . . ." Ibid., 39.

"The quest for purity. . . ." Ibid., 161.

The Re-Vision of Marginality

Page 115
"and we teach it in school all the time." For a discussion of how and why I have tried to teach law students to be "bicultural and bilingual," see my Appendix, "Sameness and Difference in a Law School Classroom: Working at the Crossroads."

Affirmative Action and Stigma

Page 119
"the *Weber* case." *United Steelworkers of America v. Weber*, 443 U.S. 193 (1979).

Page 121
"After all. . . ." Richard Rodriguez, *Hunger of Memory:*

The Education of Richard Rodriguez (Boston: David A. Godine, 1982), 169.

Page 122

"My decision was final." Ibid., 171.

"To make a poet black. . . ." Countee Cullen, "Yet Do I Marvel," in *American Negro Poetry*, ed. Arna Bontemps (Clinton, Mass.: Colonial Press, 1963), 88.

Skinwalkers, Race, and Geography

Page 129

"The Virginia legislature. . . ." Higginbotham and Kopytoff, "Racial Purity," 1978.

"Where're Your People From?"

Page 136

"a way station. . . ." John Hope Franklin, *Race and History: Selected Essays, 1938–1988* (Baton Rouge: Louisiana State University Press, 1989), 328.

An Ordinary Day

Page 141

"*Goodnight, Moon . . . The Enchanted Hair Tale.*" Margaret Wise Brown, *Goodnight, Moon* (New York: Harper & Row, 1947); Alexis De Veaux, *The Enchanted Hair Tale* (New York: Harper & Row, 1987).

Appendix: Sameness and Difference

Page 154

"The new mestiza. . . ." Gloria Anzaldúa, *Borderlands / La Frontera: The New Mestiza* (San Francisco:

Spinsters/Aunt Lute, 1987), 79–80. (Translation of the Spanish: "Her body is an intersection.")

Page 158

"Jenny Procter: Alabama." In *Lay My Burden Down: A Folk History of Slavery,* ed. Benjamin A. Botkin (Chicago: University of Chicago Press, 1945), 89.

"If You Do, They Will Kill Me." Ibid., 50.

Page 159

"Walker's poem. . . ." "Women," by Alice Walker, in *The Third Woman,* ed. Fisher, 297. Also in Alice Walker's *Revolutionary Petunias and Other Poems* (New York: Harcourt Brace, 1970).

Page 160

"Before it was over. . . ." Richard Kluger, *Simple Justice* (New York: Knopf, 1975), 3.

Page 161

"Awakenings. . . ." *Awakenings: 1954–1956* (Alexandria, Va.: PBS Video, 1986), film.

Page 162

"A howling, shrieking crowd. . . ." Relman Morin, "Black Monday," in Wilson and Jane Cassels Record, *Little Rock, U.S.A.* (San Francisco: Chandler Publishing Co., 1960), 59.

"A Fly in Buttermilk." James Baldwin, in his *Nobody Knows My Name* (New York: Dial Press, 1961), 83–97.

"*Common Ground.*" J. Anthony Lukas, *Common Ground* (New York: Knopf and Random House, 1985), 3–44.

Page 163

"as long ago as 1840. . . ." Arthur O. White, "The Black Movement Against Jim Crow Education in Buffalo, New York, 1800–1900," *Phylon* 30 (1969): 375.

Page 167
Cox v. Louisiana, 379 U.S. 536 (1965); Chicago v. Gregory, 394 U.S. 111 (1969).

Page 168
"black laws of Virginia. . . ." Guild, Black Laws of Virginia, passim.

"the film Ain't Scared. . . ." Ain't Scared of Your Jails: 1960–61 (Alexandria, Va.: PBS Video, 1986), film.

Page 171
"As I observed all this. . . ." Michael D. Gurwitz, November 7, 1989 (unpublished essay, quoted by permission).

Page 172
"Allen's book . . ." Paula Gunn Allen, The Sacred Hoop: Recovering the Feminine in American Indian Traditions (Boston: Beacon Press, 1986).

Lyng v. Northwest Indian Cemetery Protective Assoc., 485 U.S. 439 (1988); Employment Division v. Smith, 494 U.S. 872 (1990).

Page 174
"The reporter presented. . . ." Juan Forero, "Push Builds for Women, Minorities in Homicide Jobs," Buffalo News, March 21, 1992, Sec. C, p. 1.

Page 176
Pregnant but Equal (New York: Women's Film Project, 1982), film.

Page 178
"This is my daily mask. . . ." Mitsuye Yamada, "Masks of Woman," in her Desert Run: Poems and Stories (Latham, N.Y.: Kitchen Table, Women of Color Press, 1988), 89.

Page 179
"Audre Lorde's troubling essay. . . ." "Eye to Eye: Black Women, Hatred, and Anger," in Audre Lorde, Sister Outsider (Trumansburg, N.Y.: Crossing Press, 1984), 145.

"I also included a picture. . . ." William L. Katz, *Black Indians* (New York: Atheneum, 1986), frontispiece.

Page 182

"Privilege . . . spreads a thick layer. . . ." Chinua Achebe, "The Truth of Fiction," in his *Hopes and Impediments: Selected Essays* (New York: Anchor Books, 1988), 49.

Page 183

"I always challenge. . . ." Samuel R. Miserindino Jr., April 5, 1991 (unpublished essay quoted by permission).

Page 184

"new consciousness. . . ." Anzaldúa, *Borderlands*, 80.

Acknowledgments

An earlier version of "Commonalities: On Being Black and White, Different, and the Same" was published by the *Yale Journal of Law and Feminism* 2 (1990): 290ff. The same journal also published an earlier version of "Sameness and Difference in the Law School Classroom: Working at the Crossroads" (4 [1992]: 415ff.). I am grateful to the students who worked on the Journal for encouraging my work and for providing such good editorial help.

I also thank the James A. Magavern Fund of Buffalo, New York, for supporting my work on this book during the summer of 1993, and Dr. Anna Evans, for giving me permission to describe her "Mo' Black" Theory of Adaptation.

I owe a real debt of gratitude to the many friends, family members, students, and colleagues who believed in me before I believed in myself, and who encouraged me to write and to keep on writing. I also thank all those who taught me so much by sharing their stories and their lives with me. In a very real sense, this book is theirs too.

And finally, let me thank Sandy Thatcher at Penn State Press, who understood what I was trying to say and helped me say it better.

Permissions Acknowledgments

"Desmet, Idaho, March 1969" by Janet Campbell. Reprinted with permission of Kenneth Rosen, ed., *Voices of the Rainbow*, New York: Arcade Publishers, 1993.

The selection from LUCILLE CLIFTON, "some dreams hang in the air," © 1987 by Lucille Clifton. Reprinted from GOOD WOMAN: POEMS AND A MEMOIR 1969–1980, by Lucille Clifton, with the permission of BOA Editions, Ltd., 92 Park Ave., Brockport, NY 14420.

The selection from "Just Because" by Lorna C. Hill, is reprinted from *Yalla Bitch* with permission. Copyright © 1986 by Lorna C. Hill.

"Women" from *Revolutionary Petunias and Other Poems,* copyright © 1970 by Alice Walker, reprinted by permission of Harcourt Brace & Company and David Higham Associates Ltd.

The selection from "The Best?" by April Walker is reprinted from *Cabbages and Kings* (Spring 1983) with permission. © 1983 by April Walker.

Selection from "Masks of Woman" by Mitsuye Yamada from *Desert Run Poems and Stories*. © 1988 by Mitsuye Yamada and Kitchen Table: Women of Color Press. Used by permission of the author and of Kitchen Table: Women of Color Press, P.O. Box 980, Latham, N.Y. 12110.